D1483238

History of the RESTITUTION FUND COMMISSION of the Episcopal Diocese of Pennsylvania

A Challenge

EPISCOPAL
CHURCH

Other books by J. Rupert Picott:

History of the Virginia Teachers Association
—Published May 1, 1975

Walter Washington In Washington
(with Milton Williams and Dave Ogburn)
—Published January 1, 1976

The Black Experience In Elementary and Secondary Education, 1950-1975
—Published September 1, 1976

National Historic Marker
Black American Pioneers,
Part One
—Publication date, February 1, 1977

History of the RESTITUTION FUND COMMISSION of the Episcopal Diocese of Pennsylvania

A Challenge

by
J. Rupert Picott
and
Walter N. Ridley

Library of Congress Catalog Card Number 76-27967

PRINTED IN THE UNITED STATES OF AMERICA.

Picott, J. Rupert and Ridley, Walter N.

History of the Restitution Fund Commission of the Episcopal Diocese of Pennsylvania

Washington, D.C.: Restitution Fund Commission of the Episcopal Diocese of Pennsylvania.

240 p.
761Ø
76Ø727

Contents

Dedication

"People dealing with people" is the work of the Episcopal Church, and has been for hundreds of years. More recently (1970), the Diocese of Pennsylvania expressed its deep concern for human values in the "propagation of the faith" through the Restitution Fund Commission. This book is dedicated to the Diocese and to all those who "use their Christianity" to make a difference in the lives of other men, women and children.

Preface

The writing of the history of the Restitution Fund Commission of the Episcopal Diocese of Pennsylvania is in "fulfillment of the record."

The R.F.C. and its work represent for the Episcopal Diocese of Pennsylvania an effort to follow the lead of the Episcopal Church in the U.S. as well as the expressed conscience of the Bishop, many of the leaders and parishioners. This decision was the action of the Diocese in a Special Convention, called for the purpose of deciding what the church should do in response to inequalities, racism, prejudice and segregation.

The handling of all monies, and particularly the sum of half a million dollars, demanded the "responsibility of the written record." It is in response to the call of fiscal responsibility as well as human performance that this history is offered. Without this accounting, years from now there could be some questions even by some members of the Commission themselves of "what was it we did," "when" and "how." With the facts reduced to paper, the report is forever.

Let the fact and the action speak. On that high note, this account of the Restitution Fund Commission of the Diocese of Pennsylvania of the Protestant Episcopal Church begins.

Statement

This book is the combined thinking, planning and projection of the Restitution Fund Commission members, author, co-author, the numerous persons interviewed, and others who contributed in so many ways. This disclaimer is owed to all these individuals. I, J. Rupert Picott, am responsible for the content, including sections and statements on members of the Commission.

Acknowledgment

The authors are indebted to so many persons for assistance that "we dare not call names."

Suffice it to say, a debt is owed to all of the members of the Restitution Fund Commission; to a host of priests in the Episcopal Church in the Diocese of Pennsylvania; to members of the Church, particularly the Diocese of Pennsylvania, who "hold no office, nor yearn for any position;" and to hundreds of others who helped in many ways. The authors are grateful to all.

Because they labored so diligently and "caught the flack" on those days when words did not come easily, let us single out the entire staff of the Association for the Study of Afro-American Life and History, headquartered in Washington, D.C.

To Miss Evangeline Chambers, and Mrs. Rae Reccuiti, who took the dictation and transferred "the oral statements to the written record" and made sense with the words, we owe special plaudits.

Comment

The process by which the Restitution Fund Committee provided assistance with the funds on hand was a major concern of the Commission members.

To achieve the ends stated in the philosophy expressed by the Commission there followed naturally, "evaluation, re-evaluation, and further re-evaluation." This process of growth aided the Commission's performance substantially, and accordingly, is highlighted throughout this report.

Chapter I

The Reverend Absolom Jones

A founder of the Church in America.

The Church of the Advocate, Episcopal, located in Inner-City, Philadelphia.

Saga of a church in action. . . .

This is a report of a Church's seeking-searching. . . its response to pleas from its members for a new human conceptual stance, for the creation of a new match of the establishment listening, for a change in thinking from the philanthropic, minimal "loosening of belt," to a genuine consideration of man in need. It is not an asking to submit the man helped to a barrage of feelings that would tend to lower human dignity. It is a look at the basic consideration of living that lifts man into the realm fostered from ancient days of the Church that the human is the "highest form of living."

The Church as an institution, often grown fat in pecuniary acquisition as well as the purple trappings, is well known for conservatism. Indeed, many contend that rather than change, the Church is society's most formidable bastion of tradition. The records show that many fighters within the Church strove, valiantly and militantly, without basically changing priest or priestly abode or priestly written Biblical wordings.

If this be the situation with the Church, immaculate and universal, the origins of the Episcopal denomination show little or no variation. The Episcopal Church got from the Mother Church at Rome a face steeped deeply in tradition and folklore, which required not only the Biblical subservience of its adherents, but pounds to support its existence. From its beginnings, the Church of England insisted upon much of the embodiment of the Roman Church with the claim of ancestry from the Disciple Peter. The Episcopal Church, later transplanted to America, was changed very little either "in the doing" or the "Biblical structure" upon which it based its action. It is not without reason, then, that the Episcopal Church is grounded "part and parcel" in the "centuries of its progenitor." To be sure, before and after the 1776 beginnings of the United States nation, the Episcopalian found it helpful in the "wilderness of the new land" to "hang on tenaciously to old customs and ingrained habits" of the past. Thus, was living made less difficult.

Another major factor must be kept in mind. It is if "change is the attribute of the young," direction of the Church was generally counted the property of the older. So those who would fashion a new institution often ran smack into the "wall of the go slow." The written practices in the Church were frequently defended by those who found procedures followed comfortable.

In the thousands of years of development of the long struggle for dominance of populist thought, confrontation was most often the "way of the movement." So it was with the Church of England's offspring, directly in America and especially in Pennsylvania. The record is replete with demands "to do something about something" held dear to the hearts of the doers. It is, thus, our story of the Restitution Fund Commission of the Episcopal Church, Diocese of Pennsylvania, product of the 1950-1975 "period of radical change" in America, begins.

Chapter II

Holy Communion Church, Episcopal, Neighborhood Youth Center.

Headquarters of the Restitution Fund Commission.

When all of America was inflamed. . . .

Our presentation of the Episcopal movement, and particularly of the restitution effort, is within the context of the past quarter century and it is to this story that we now turn. The members of the Episcopal Church, like all Americans, were not immune to the thrusts, sometimes violent and at other times less in the fighting spirit, in this period when all of America was inflamed. During these years when the American people entered a new era, John F. Kennedy talked poignantly: "Ask not what your country can do for you, ask what you can do for your country." There were "dreams," and "the dreamers caught up in the dream" were willing to give their lives to make things better. . . and sometimes, unfortunately, death was the price. Despite these drawbacks, despite the lethargy of centuries of non-movement, despite the tug of the status quo, and despite the frailties of both those who would go forward and those who would hold back, and despite the satisfaction of the known versus the imagined dangers of the unknown, there grew during this quarter century a significant cadre of Americans who gave meaning to the dream.

The twenty-five year period has been labelled by "stylists of the written word" as the "Quarter Century of the Revolution." More properly, the years since the Brown vs. Topeka Supreme Court integration decision may be designated the "Period of Minority Thrust"—the young, the Black, the Indian, the poor white, women—all groups previously not in the establishment structure, regardless of population size or potential. The impact of these forces may be dulled, but in their places there are war, the astounding revelations of the American CIA operations at home and abroad, the resignation of a President of the United States and the subsequent pardon to evade moral charges, and the ousting of a Vice-President of the same administration. These have brought reaction, frustration, and fury unknown and unparalleled in the history of so powerful a democracy. Moreover, the American people had brought to attention—although many did not hear or believe—the alienation and injustice of the American way for substantial segments of our population.

Greensboro, where the remonstrance took form; Montgomery, where the movement acquired dynamics; Birmingham, where the revolution flowered; Berkeley, where the protest burgeoned; and Detroit, where riots symbolized urban crisis were intimately part of these remarkable years. Confrontations with the torch in Watts, Newark, Washington, D.C.; the college student involvement at Columbia, San Francisco State, Cornell and Harvard; and the sudden confidential strides by thousands of leaders in hundreds of cities and towns across the land added dimension to the struggle.

The list of those who cared for freedom and acted in those years is well known. Martin Luther King and the two Kennedys were victims of assassins' bullets. Many blacks, symbolized by Roy Wilkins and Thurgood Marshall, linking human rights to the Constitution, and by Stokeley Carmichael and Rap Brown, replaced in leadership; Lyndon B. Johnson, forced, by his choice of Vietnam, to choose not to run again for the presidency, were also in the phalanx of many who took mighty swipes at segregation's bastions.

Then a new, powerful force came to the fore. This so-called silent majority was, as always, often used as a damper on human progress.

As could be expected, numerous action power bases were recognized and developed. The slogans—Black Power, Youth Power, Brown Power, and Women Power—became rather well respected. Although there existed a built-in fear of even the word "power," the exertion of power as a legitimate instrument for change was gradually accepted.

Some other things during the past twenty-five years changed in substance and it was upon these new behavioral phenomena that much of the future depends for many people. Included are tremendously important concepts and action oriented designs:

1. The conceptualization that "Black is beautiful" was believed. Perhaps no verbalism in modern times so dramatically altered the emotional self-vision of a whole people.
2. Black became a term of respectability. Black became a badge of pride. It was a heady appeal to self-concept. It was the answer, at last, to tens of thousands of commencement orations "to believe in yourself" and, thus, "be somebody." It was the exhortation that boldly demanded proud self-identification. It was, to a black person, a reminder that the blood of ancient fathers runs in the veins.

But out of this time of revolution, hope developed—evidence that America could be better, even if there were scarcely ripples:

1. The new-found faith of the young, the black and the disenchanted in themselves as change agents in the struggles with the establishment continued, and this self-concept is the bright horizon of the years ahead.

2. The clamor for a rightful piece of the action became louder, and hope that segregated unions and segregated businesses would be forced to listen and grant blacks, women, and the young jobs, opportunity for business management and ownership, abounded.

Before more than 250,000 in the 1963 March on Washington, the preacher Martin Luther King declared, "I have a dream..." To many who were optimistic, there was still the hope that "one day this nation will rise up, and live out the true meaning of its creed."

This was the "water" in which the Episcopalians of the Diocese of Pennsylvania "waded," however timidly... and it is from this circumstance and circumspection that the black minority demanded of their white brethren a "new kind of trend," a "new kind of response" and a "new kind of fulfillment" in the Church of Christ in the Diocese of Pennsylvania.

The Most Reverend John E. Hines, Presiding Bishop, 1965-1974, Protestant Episcopal Church of the United States of America.

Chapter III

. . . right off the fields of the "long hot summer. . . ."

The national convention of the Episcopal Church held in Seattle came right off the fields of the "long hot summer."

This 1967 national meeting of the Church could not keep to the quiet, usual methods of "saving souls" and of reporting on priestly conduct and membership support over the previous four years. There was too much happening at the very doors of the convention. Activists clamored for attention. Their tactics harkened back to ancient days of the street fighters for democracy on the boulevards of Paris shouting "liberté, égalité, and fraternité," of John Brown's Harpers Ferry dramatic "do or die" stand for freedom of the slaves and of Mohandas K. Ghandi's non-violent protest in Africa and India.

These purveyors of better human relationships, like their previous goal-setters and a host of others, going backwards in time, made their mark on the "conscience of man." They appealed for "human sanity" and some Americans listened.

We turn now to Bishop Hines and his "report to the mind" and "plea to the soul" at the Seattle convention. The Bishop had taken the summer off just before the convention and visited Watts in Los Angeles, 14th Street in Washington, the streets numbered in the hundreds in Harlem, and the ghetto areas of North Philadelphia. This presiding officer of the National Episcopal Church had seen personally and first-hand the agitation for change in the lackadaisical, alien American black/white people relations. The Bishop came away from the inner cities deeply and personally involved, and sensing a new relationship between prayers, preaching and practices. He talked with feeling at the Seattle convention, presented his call for action with clarity, and urged the men and women of the Episcopal Church to respond to the need with fervor.

The words of the presiding Bishop at Seattle are memorable, constitute the basis for action within the Church, and provide sanction from the national officer seldom found in the annals of the denomination. But we must let presiding Bishop Hines speak for himself. Some of his moving words follow:

WORSHIP AT THE GENERAL CONVENTION

Opening Service

(The General Convention of 1967 opened with Choral Evening Prayer in the Coliseum, Seattle Center, Seattle, Washington, on September 17, at 8:00 o'clock.

The Vice-Chairman of the House of Bishops, the Rt. Rev. Nelson M. Burroughs, D.D., officiated. The Lessons were read, respectively, by the Secretary of the House of Bishops, the Rt. Rev. Scott Field Bailey, D.D., and the Secretary of the House of Deputies, the Rev. Canon Charles M. Guilbert, S.T.D.

The Presiding Bishop, the Rt. Rev. John E. Hines, D.D., preached the General Convention Sermon, which concluded with a call to the Church, on the subject of the *Crisis in American Life*, as follows:

"As Presiding Bishop of this Church, by God's help I trust, and with the help of others—some not of this Church—I have tried to hear what God may be saying to the Churches in the crisis in American cities.

"Extreme actions on the part of a dispossessed people bespeaks a conviction that white man's justice is no justice for the black man, particularly those trapped in the ghettos of this land. And many of them have despaired of attaining that justice through structures and institutions which they see as channels of the white man's power. The grim consequences of the rioting indicate a tenaciously held conviction that any relief that comes will have to come by acquisition of, or seizure of, sufficient power on their part to enable them to shape their own destiny, taking their place equally alongside other men. This they are prepared to do—even if they have to die in the attempt. Further, and this touches us at a sensitive point, these unfortunate people—many of them—have written off the Churches as possible allies in their quest for justice, for they have seen little concrete evidence that Church people are concerned about their plight or will take the necessary risk to help redeem it.

"In trying to hear what is being said in the confusion of our time, I have walked—a little bit—in the ghetto-areas of four of our cities. I can only tell you what I know—know from an unrehearsed face-to-face confrontation with black people, some militant leftists., others solidly moderate—most of them bearing in their souls (and some on their bodies) the indignities and brutality which have erupted in anger and rebellion. I recruited a task-force of our own staff, together with competent outside advisers. I requested the counsel of a group of ghetto leaders in exploring the question: 'How can the resources of this Church, resources human and financial, be enlisted intelligently and humbly in the service of the people of the cities; and by what criterion can this Church enter into partnership with the indigenous community-groups in impoverished slum-areas which have been organized by the residents themselves, are run by them, and are seeking to alleviate the conditions which are destroying them?'

"I believe that people in all walks of life, Churchmen in our own land and abroad, the people from whom hope is being squeezed out, want to know where we, as Christians, stand—and whether our position is manifested in deeds that cannot be misunderstood.

"As at least the beginning of this Church's response to the deep human need dramatized by the confiict in the cities, I am recommending the development of a program, to be extended over the next triennium, by which this Church can take its place, humbly and boldly, alongside, and in support of, the dispossessed and oppressed peoples of this country, for the healing of our national life. Among its aims will be the bringing of people in ghettos into areas of decision-making by which their destiny is influenced. It will encourage the use of political and economic power to support justice and self-determination for all men. It will make available skilled personnel-assistance, and request the appropriation of substantial sums of money to community-organizations involved in the betterment of depressed urban areas, and under the control of those who are largely both black and poor, that their power for self-determination may be increased and their dignity restored. It is suggested that these efforts be administered through coalitions with other Churches and agencies such as the Inter-Religious Foundation for Community Organization, that we may be joined with and by other groups in similar efforts directed toward the same goals.

"I am requesting the funding of such a program in the amount of approximately $3 million annually; such funds to be secured from various sources, principally from the General Church Program.

"Finally, a re-ordering of primary emphases and priority-ratings in the proposed General Program will be required, in order to support the programmatic response outlined here.

"I am requesting the General Convention and the Triennial of the Women of the Church to create appropriate committees to review this call to action by your Presiding Bishop and the Executive Council and charging them to make such recommendations as may seem wise to them in the light of the critical nature of the need. I am sure that means for mutual discussion and co-operation between these committees can be found by such ingenious and creative personnel.

"But I would heavily underline a word of caution: no matter what this Church at the national level may decide we can do, both in human and financial terms, it will be only a token, a symbol, if, perhaps happily, a sacrament. What we do here can never be more than an "earnest", pointing to the necessity for, and the effectiveness of, a sensitive and sacrificial response on the part of the people of the Church. For, unless our men, women, and young people enlist in patterns of diocesan, parish, and mission engagement, which involves them personally as well as financially, even the best effort at this level will prove fruitless.

"What is before us is not primarily a matter of money. Money can help if we take our hands off its control, giving it because we realize that it is God's and not ours. But if we attempt to use money to "buy our way" out of responsibility, the less credible we will appear to men and women struggling with their misery, and the less likely we are to build our part of a bridge between our alienations. Perhaps we can understand a little that it is only through our sharing in the pain and agonized frustration of the dispossessed that our own renewal can come to be.

"I hope that this plea for a corporate response of Episcopalians will not have to stand alone. We are too small a group, and our resources—even if given freely—are far too limited to cope successfully with the crisis in our city streets. I hope I am not presumptuous in appealing to the nation-wide community of faith—to our Jewish brethren, to our Christian brethren—Roman Catholic, Orthdox and Protestant—to join together with us in a bold, full-scale, mobilization of our resources that can be dedicated to the righting of a great wrong and the healing of a bleeding wound in the body of our nation's life. For it may be that we are in "a moment of passing grace" given to us by God, that may never again re-occur—and in which we are given together the opportunity to act."

The Seattle convention approved the concept of the appropriation of the funds without designation. It was left to the special meeting at the University of Notre Dame in South Bend to provide the guidelines for how the money should be appropriated. It is to South Bend that we now turn.

Chapter IV

Muhammad Kenyatta, Director,
Black Economic Development Conference, Inc.

Barbara Harris and others at the Convention, Episcopal Church, South Bend, Indiana.

These two together—
man and idea. . . .

The historian searching for truth frequently looks for "a man and an idea." The conjoint appearance of these two—man and idea—is often the catalytic circumstance for the promotion of the great movements of the world. Christianity is one of these, the Restitution Fund Commission is another.

But our story is about the secular. It, nonetheless, concerns man and idea. The man was Muhammad Kenyatta and the idea was "help to the inner city needy people" that would make the difference.

Let us look at the scene in the South Bend gathering. The meeting had droned on for sometime. Suddenly there came to the front of the hall Muhammad Kenyatta of Philadelphia. This sensitive, to some shocking, but articulate spokesman of the poor, of the depressed and of the "left out" seized the microphone and began to talk. To some of the "hold on" type in the audience, Kenyatta projected the image of "swinging from the chandeliers," but to the majority, Kenyatta came across as a diligent, bright person who was acquainted with what the gospel of our Lord Jesus Christ was all about. The longer Kenyatta talked, the more he gained respect for himself and for his idea.

Barbara Harris, a determined lady, with all of her 96 pounds, was close by, figuratively standing in the aisle to keep 2,000 people from disturbing Kenyatta as he gave his presentation of "need" and of "helping those in need." Ms. Harris was aided and supported by laymen, priests and students, black and white.

It soon became obvious that as Kenyatta listed demands, which he offered eloquently, a whole cadre of black and white people nodded "Amen." They thus showed the convention that they were behind this man and his idea of reparations.

Muhammad Kenyatta in his South Bend presentation had subsequently demonstrated to all a knowledge of the historical unresponsiveness of the Episcopal Church to human issues where black people were concerned. Kenyatta did not say so, but he must have been aware of the statements of many, as exemplified from the following.

The prevailing temper of the Protestant Episcopal Church in Revolutionary times is this testified of by John Jay, Esq., of the city of New York—himself an Episcopalian—in a pamphlet entitled *"Thoughts on the duty of the Episcopal Church in relation to slavery"*:

> Alas! for the expectation that she would conform to the spirit of her ancient mother! She has not merely remained a mute and careless spectator of this great conflict of truth and justice with hypocrisy and cruelty, but her very priests and deacons may be seen ministering at the altar of slavery, offering their talents and influence at its unholy shrine... whatever they may feel upon this subject, rebuke it neither in public nor in private; and her periodicals, far from advancing the progress of abolition, at times oppose our societies, impliedly defending slavery, as not incompatible with Christianity, and occasionally withholding information useful to the cause of freedom.

In an article in the *Christian Century* in 1931, Dr. William E.B. DuBois declared:

> "The church, as a whole, insists on a divine mission and guidance and the indisputable possession of truth. Is there anything in the record of the church in America in regard to the Negro to prove this? There is not. If the treatment of the Negro by the Christian Church is called 'divine', this is an attack on the conception of God more blasphemous than any which the church has always been so ready and eager to punish."

In 1959 Liston Pope of Yale Divinity School wrote of Protestantism:

> Its record indicates clearly that the church is the most segregated major institution in American society. It has lagged behind the Supreme Court as the conscience of the nation on questions of race, and it has fallen far behind trade unions, factories, schools, department stores, athletic gatherings, and most other areas of human association as far as the achievements of integration in its own life is concerned.

Muhammad Kenyatta Disrupts and Challenges the General Convention at South Bend

Muhammad Kenyatta reports that he and Wilmer Woodland, associate director of the Black Economic Development Conference, chose to approach the general convention of the Protestant Episcopal Church at South Bend for two reasons. First, they felt the irresistible urge of the Black Manifesto. Second, they felt it imperative to have a forum in order to reach the larger church in America. He felt that the Episcopal Diocese of Pennsylvania, and especially the blacks in this diocese, had been responsive to this cause and could be depended upon to help get the message across.

Kenyatta states that there was no plan of action. He did not know enough about the convention plan to develop one. Shortly after arrival in South Bend, he participated in a religious service with the young Episcopalians who were at the convention, found that they were impatient with much in the church and the convention. Together the young leaders and Kenyatta agreed that the young people would support Kenyatta's efforts to be heard at the convention, and that they would come to the place where the effort to be heard would be made barefoot to symbolize that "this ground is holy ground" and to induce the convention to hear, through Kenyatta, the plight and call of the blacks.

From unexpected quarters—from priests and laymen, from women, from young people, from the Black Caucus—came words and acts of support. Meanwhile, on the convention floor was an extended discussion about the training and placement of priests. Much of the discussion had to do with the fact that the training and placement had not been applied equally to black and white priests. Finally, after what he describes as a religious experience of singing spirituals, crying and soul-searching, Kenyatta and his friend decided that since efforts of several leaders at the convention and himself in requesting time to speak to the convention had been to no avail, the convention must be disrupted. . . . The time came and, he reports, "we went up to the podium surrounded by young people, some laymen and clergy, black and white." He said to Bishop Hines, "Sir, we want to present the Manifesto—we want time to be heard." The Bishop said, "Muhammad, behave!" Kenyatta insisted that he "must be heard about the pain and suffering and the history behind why we are where we are today." He seized the microphone, but returned it to the Bishop when he said he would listen. He asked the convention whether he could be given time. Then ensued a lengthy discussion as to whether time should be granted. After statements on both sides of the issue, ten minutes were granted by a simple majority vote.

Kenyatta felt frustrated that after all of the labor and time spent in getting to this point he was given only ten minutes. He explained the concept of reparations, how reparations relate to restitution and "my understanding of the Gospel, which says that you must recognize things that have been done, and make restitution before you can talk about reconciliation."

"I tried to share with people the anger and anguish of 400 years of suffering. I said, 'You have chopped our legs out from under us socially and economically, and then you say we have equality. We have crippled legs. You have healthy legs. Now you tell us to run and keep up with you.'" He said "We had a real interest in material support, but wanted to cause the Church to realize how they were treating their black brothers and sisters in their own church." Finally, he said, "If you cannot love your brother whom you have seen, how can you claim to love the Lord whom you have not seen."

Kenyatta reports that he felt a response from the people in the convention, although he felt that most of them did not know much about the Manifesto, and had no clear theological sense of the concept of restitution, he conceived. Although he thought many conceived his appearance as that of a ghetto group "marching in with machine guns like bank robbers," he felt a relief of tension as he perceived that people were feeling as if "we were human beings, and were trying to share and explain the anger which is based upon some of the insensitivity that the Church had been displaying even to its own black communicants."

Kenyatta reports that there were some attempts on the part of black and white officials of the church to capitalize upon the circumstance and to get increased money for pet projects or "to open up this or that for blacks." However, he indicates that the proper course which he was recommending was for the Church to give credibility and legitimacy to the guidance and participation of blacks in the Church and to make some decisions about their own welfare and destiny. This to be supported by the transferral of funds to legitimate groups within the Church, who would make reparations and restitution, thereby effecting reconciliation.

The Pennsylvania militant Civil Rights leader's pungent and shrill words in South Bend wrought better than he perhaps realized. He charted a "path" directly to Philadelphia. It is this development that we now record.

Chapter V

The Right Reverend Robert L. Dewitt, Bishop, Diocese of Pennsylvania, The Episcopal Church, 1964–1974.

The lady: Mattie Humphrey.

. . . . *"No, Bishop, we've got a problem."*

The lady was an intelligent, well-dressed black American and the time was about 1965. The Right Reverend Robert L. Dewitt, then the Bishop of the Diocese of Pennsylvania, and the lady were engaged in a meaningful conversation. The Bishop asked, "Madame, what do you think of the riots that have taken place in certain parts of the country?" "Riots, Bishop?" the lady responded. She continued, "those riots were only a coming out party!"

The Reverend Paul Washington, at the Bishop's request, had called a number of "movers and shakers" to the Church of the Advocate in inner-city Philadelphia to share their experiences and hopefully to sharpen the Bishop's insights into the causes for unrest. Ms. Mattie Humphrey was a member of the group. Eloquent, cogent and informative statements about the meaning of the riots for better human relations, the division they would cause, and some suggestions for dealing with the situation were offered. Ms. Humphrey had to leave early and the Bishop went to the door to help her with her coat. Ms. Humphrey said upon leaving, "Bishop, you've got a problem." After pausing, she said, "No, Bishop, we've got a problem!"

The Bishop had opened the session by putting one question to the group and then moved back in the corner. He listened for about three hours while the conversation, sometimes strident, at other times less abrasive, whirled around. The group, because Father Washington had called them and they believed in him, felt that they could express their thoughts freely. They pulled few punches and differed with each other, but always there was a need expressed for "action"... and "action now."

The Bishop declared in an interview that the session was a "considerable education" for him and he meant it. There was not unanimity among the group, but what most often came to the fore was the urgent plea that white Episcopalians "should hear the simple language, the beliefs, interpretations, and conclusions" of the citizens of the Philadelphia inner-city as to what the church was doing and what needed to be done.

Many of those present lingered after the formal session had been ended. What was most in the minds of the Bishop and of all present was the "obligation of the Episcopal Church." The scripture seemed so pertinent:

> "Who so hath this world's goods and seeth that his brother hath need and shutteth up his bowels and compassion from them, how dwelleth the love of God in him?"

Chapter VI

Norman P. Harburger

Father Richard Hawkins of St. Thomas' Church, Whitemarsh.

. . . bogged in the inertia of delay
and in the fear of action.

Our story moves logically to the Diocesan Convention in 1969.

The history of action by the Episcopal Diocese of Pennsylvania to assist in black determination and to help black identity was in part, in the early days, the work of the Hawkins' Committee, appointed by Bishop Dewitt in the Summer of 1969 to recommend responsible actions for the Diocese relevant to the black conditions and demands. The Committee made what came to be known as the Hawkins Report at the Diocesan Convention of October 1969.

The Hawkins report asked the Church to move positively and immediately on the appropriations of funds for a new human relations stance. The program would assist numerous projects for blacks within the Church structure and particularly in the inner city.

It appeared for a time in the Diocesan Convention that nothing would be done because the whole matter of financial assistance for human relations was bogged down "in the inertia of delay and in the fear of action."

Norman Harburger came to the rescue. Mr. Harburger, a suburban Philadelphia businessman and public relationist, drafted a resolution which took Hawkins Report "off of dead center." The Harburger resolution called for the creation of a Task Force on Reconciliation.

The Task Force, by its very nature, provided for study, but it also opened the way for action. The white and some black conservatives in the Diocesan Convention, and the black proponents of increased Church involvement in human relations both "bought" the Task Force. The resolution passed.

The scene was so reminiscent of a similar period centuries ago. The words of Victor Hugo are "Nothing is so powerful as an idea whose time has come."

Mr. Harburger had "saved the day" and his effort became widely known as the "Harburger Resolution." The real work of finding money for drafting a program and getting that program accepted by the Diocese of Pennsylvania had yet to be achieved.

Chapter VII

Before.

After.

. . . Buy Us, As Well as the Bold Program

Bishop Dewitt, with accustomed clarity and empathy, immediately appointed Norman Harburger chairman of the Task Force. Harburger shrewdly suggested other persons, including Charlie Ritchie, chairman of the Diocese and John Butterworth who was Vice Chancellor of the Diocese at the time.

Bishop Dewitt, Norman Harburger and others who constituted the Task Force on Reconciliation knew well that the period was turbulent and highly emotionally charged.

The Task Force accepted the challenge. After the first session, the group reported to the Bishop that this was one of the most exciting things that they had had the opportunity to undertake.

The Task Force set for itself a report date of "early in 1970, by June at the latest." Within the Task Force, May 1970 became the target date for a report to the entire Diocese.

The Task Force started in February. A "divorced" group of people brought together around controversial issues met each Monday night from 5:30 p.m. to 9:30 p.m. for a period of four months. The attendance was an unbelievable eighty per cent or better: There were also smaller meetings of sub-committees on many Saturdays.

As the Task Force Report began to take shape, numerous persons and groups outside the Task Force asked for information. The Task Force realized that this was an excellent vehicle to get their message across to the people. Members of the Task Force participated in eleven meetings to interpret the program.

Mr. Harburger, and the other members of the Task Force had keen public relations understanding. The group decided that they would "pull together" a program that the members could support personally. On this basis, the group agreed further to urge the people of the Diocese to "buy us" as well as the "bold program," a program bold, at least, by previous Episcopal Church standards.

A tremendous learning experience and working amalgamation took place within the Task Force itself. There were persons like Mary Jane Baker, bright middle-aged liberalist white woman; Bruce Beal, young white person; Barbara Belcher, a teenager and liberal; Bern Bowers, middle-class, "hard hat" oriented; Father B. Campbell, a little to the liberal side; Father Michael Campbell, a "middle-of-the-road," white clergyman; Al Dorsey, a conservative black person; Father Robert DuBose, an action-oriented, liberal, black clergyman; Jack Fair, an elderly gentleman and retired purchasing agent of the Pennsylvania Railroad for whom this experience was a human relations first; Mrs. Bette Forrester, a conservative black churchwoman; the Reverend Kenneth Grannum, a high churchman, probably leaning toward the conservative; Pamela Horn, a black teenager and very effective; The Reverend Dave Hyde, a white conservative; Frank Ennis, one of the less faithful members, a "middle-of-the-road" white school student; Harold Pilgrim, a conservative black man and high churchman; John Platt, moderate; Dr. Walter N. Ridley, a "middle-of-the-roader," a little to the left of the active conservative spectrum among blacks; William Scott, of the Frankford Arsenal, a "middle-of-the-road" black man; Walter Spatoff, a conservative white realtor; Mrs. Carol Stone, liberal white woman; and Mrs. Helen White, white middle-class woman.

The Task Force meetings provided a communications basis within the Church, while personally demanding time and frequent emotional draining, nonetheless set the foundation for a new kind of black/white working together within the Diocese of Pennsylvania. The Committee's report to which we now allude was a merging of diverse thinking, a merging of long-held traditions and effusion of Christ-like concepts within the Christiandom of the Diocese. The Diocese owes a debt of gratitude to Norman Harburger and the entire Task Force for perception and vision and tenacity.

The Harburger Task Force meetings were sometimes punctuated by surprise. agitation, transference, projection and straying from the issue "at hand." It was then that the chairman would quote from the famed message of St. Paul and bring the session to focus:

> ". . . in Christ there is neither Jew or Greek, neither bound nor free, but all one in Christ."

Chapter VIII

November, 1963 THE CHURCH NEWS

FROM PLAYGR...-14 year-olds who registered at day camp at closed-of... area. All had t... meeting of counselors who moved result was 32 comm... photo at right, 22 fulfilled the... nts present.

The Evening Bulletin
PHILADELPHIA Friday, April 3, 1964

Residents Critical of Police At N. Phila. Town Meeting

By MARTIN HERMAN
Of The Bulletin Staff

Deputy Police Commissioner Richard T. Edwards told a North Philadelphia town meeting last night that people just don't appreciate the Police Department.

"We're doing a very good job, if I have to say so myself."

And he did say so himself.

For the next 45 minutes he had to listen to most of the 300 persons at the meeting complain about the department.

The meeting was held in the Church of the Advocate, 18th and Diamond sts.

Mrs. Jane Jackson, of 201... Van Pelt st., said teen-ager... wait until a patrol car passe... before they commit crimes.

"We need more policeme... here," she said. "We need t... bring back the foot patrolme... There are just too many rob... beries."

Cites Heavy Protection

Edwards replied that Nort... Central Philadelphia has mo... police protection than any othe... section of the city.

"This area has an average o... two and a quarter policemen fo... every 1,000 people," Edwa... said. "That's twice as many p...

. Paul Washington:

...piscopal P... ...uman Rel...

...Commission on Human Re... was back at full strength ...week (Jan. 14) with the ap...ment of Rev. Paul M. Wash... to the one existing vacancy ...appointment by Mayor James...

...Tate followed by a day th... ...of attorney Sydney C. O... ...to the Commission.

...Washington, 42, is rector ...(Episcopal) Church of the Ad...te, 18th and Diamond sts. He ...native of Charleston, S. C., ...te of Lincoln (Pa.) Univer... and the Philadelphia Divinity ...ol, and is married and has ...children.

...v. Washington has worked ...the Commission in resolving ...ing problems in Eastwick and...

...G. JUNE 29, 1963

FIRE AT HOSPITAL SITE

About 30 persons, left homeless by the fire, were taken to the Church of the Advocate, 18th and Diamond sts. for emergency shelter. Red Cross workers helped them find clothing and more permanent lodgings.

Fire Friday afternoon damaged a wooden shed containing bags of cement and plaster on a construction site at Broad and Ritner sts., where a wing is being built for Methodist Hospital. The blaze was extinguished in five minutes.

BISHOP ARMSTRONG

...Mary's. On May 11, 1949, he was elected Suffragan Bishop of the diocese and was consecrated in a ceremony Oct. 29 at the Memorial Church of the Advocate, 18th and Diamond...

Knife-Wielder Slain by Officer In North Phila.

Continued from First Page

...ers assisted in quieting th... neighborhood.

Paul Dandridge, of the city Commission on Human Rel...tions, and the Rev. Paul Was...ington, of the Church of t... Advocate, 18th and Diamo... sts., helped police in reassuri... the crowd. They asked everyo... to keep moving or go home.

Up F...

By HARRY G. TOLAND
Of the Editorial Page Staff

Every war has its generals in command posts to the rear and its soldiers on the front line. The "war on poverty" is no different.

One of the foxhole fighters of this conflict is the Rev. Paul M. Washington, rector of the (Episcopal) Church of the Advocate at 18th and Diamond sts. We sought him out to get his opinion on some of the strategic priorities of the "war," lately declared by President Johnson.

...e flesh," said the Rev. Paul ..., Rector of the Advocate, ...ual meeting of this parish

Advocate is 'End' For N. Phila. Gangs

Martin J. Herman, of The Bulletin staff, had a great January story on the plan to win North Philadelphia's teen-age gangs over to the work of Christ.

William Jay supervises a 24-member group that meets every Thursday at the Church of the Advocate, 18th and Diamond Sts. The "gangs" go to summer camp, hold social dances and have an annual banquet.

Allegheny Distric... Boy Scout Activiti...

The Charter presentati... to Cub Pack 525 and Boy Sc... Troop 525 will be made dur... the next Sunday morning se... ice at the Episcopal Churc... the Advocate.

The service will be condu... ed by the Rector, Rev. Paul Washington, who is serv... well as Allegheny District ... vancement Chairman.

Twenty-second District ...

— In God We Trust —

...ecture on Religious Art ... Boston Authority Feb. 16

A presentation on religious ...

A Part of the Philadelphia Scene in 1964.

Father Jesse Anderson was unofficial pastor to nationwide community of black and white Episcopalians.

From the book of Common Prayer,
the word "restitution"

The Task Force for Reconciliation moved cooperatively and diligently toward a consensus and finally prepared a report accepted by all of its members. It was considered at a Special Diocesan Convention on May 23, 1970, called for this purpose only.

In the Diocesan Convention there developed a hitch. Black leaders had asked the churches for "reparations" and Muhammad Kenyatta had emphasized the word and the concept. To many of the white and a few black persons present, and this was the majority, the more "reparations" was used the more the word seemed anathema. The schism that developed seemed formidable. The white majority of the Church did not seem to want to have it said and to admit by the use of the word "reparations" that payments were due. Moreover, it was argued, how can the present parishioners be held responsible for omission of their fathers in the Church?

Into this breach, Father Jesse Anderson stepped. Mr. Anderson, an astute politician, shrewdly sizing up the situation, declared that he "understood why you white people cannot take the word "reparations." He declared, "I'll recommend to you a word that means exactly the same thing but which is used in the book of Common Prayer and that is the word 'restitution'." Thus was born the Restitution Fund Commission.

Restitution Fund Commission members: left to right, the Reverends Charles Poindexter and William J. Johnson.

Chapter IX

Commission Members: Charles W. Polk (L) and Paul V. Gibson.

Meeting of a committee Restitution Fund Commission. Left to right: Arthur Slater, James Blake, the Reverend Thomas Logan and Mrs. Nellie A. Barnes.

. . . for work with human beings

The amount of $500,000 was referred to by some "Philadelphia street people" in the popular vernacular as "one-half a million dollars." Within the Diocese, the sum was counted small and was regarded as only the beginning "stab" to initiate the program "to solve some of the human relations" problems. The discussion by many set the ultimate amount expected at $5,000,000.00. This figure was mentioned in the Hawkins report. Though no amount was stated in the Harburger Report to the Diocese, the Harburger group indicated that it could not suggest a "top" on the amount needed.

The Diocese of Pennsylvania owned a churchhouse next to the Church of the Holy Trinity on Rittenhouse Square in Philadelphia. Sale of this property was duly authorized and made. Subsequent to the 1970 convention report to the Diocese, the amount of $500,000 was appropriated toward "work with human beings" by the Episcopal Diocese of Pennsylvania.

The appropriation for this cause was not "without its price." Many persons in the Church thought that all moneys realized from sale of capital investment should be placed in "permanent funds" for a use later in "permanent structures." These persons, and some of them were very outspoken, felt that money invested in human relations was a "one-time" answer to a problem that would undoubtedly continue for many years. To these, some faithful Episcopalians, the word permanent was an endeared term. It was the road-block used by others, sometimes expressed, but most often unuttered, that these funds should not be given to black causes and black institutions.

All the money, it seems, and especially this $500,000, became a prime target to which many zeroed. At least one leader made a proposal for most of the entire amount. Others "tooled up" for getting their hands on some of the money.

The Restitution Commission wisely refused to appropriate any money whatsoever until rules of operation could be established by the Commission and a "modus operandi" could be completed. From the very beginning, the Commission assumed that records of concept, income and expenditure should be kept, anticipating the audit usual in such church matters.

A division of considerable potential involving primarily black leaders surfaced. Some Commission members and others began to state their belief that the Restitution Fund Commission was to be only the "vehicle through which the funds were to be channelled."

A majority of the Restitution Fund Commission insisted that handling the money was a "sacred charge" and the distribution of the funds should be administered and granted after the most thorough search of the projects. In the end, this latter procedure was followed by the Commission and almost all of the cases received a complete examination and evaluation that was made first by a subcommittee and then passed by the entire Commission.

Actions of many persons became suspect. Even Bishop Dewitt was charged with encouraging the opponents of the Restitution Fund Commission's procedures. The Bishop, it was contended, favored loose controls in granting the money. In this way, it was held, the Bishop sought to demonstrate that he could work with all Episcopalians, however "far out."

One prominent Episcopalian and member of the original Task Force whose husband pledged $15,000.00 to the Restitution Fund Commission decided not to do so when she heard that there had been a "split in thinking" in the Commission. Some of the parishes who had made promises of financial support seized this talk of division within the black church community and withheld their funds.

The black communicants in the Church also did not rally to the program with gifts of money, although words were sometimes plentiful. The examination to which we now turn this spotlight, although limited by these factors, is a report of a tremendous undertaking operating during Black Manifesto days. How the Restitution Fund Commission geared up to do the job it assigned to itself, we now examine.

Chapter X

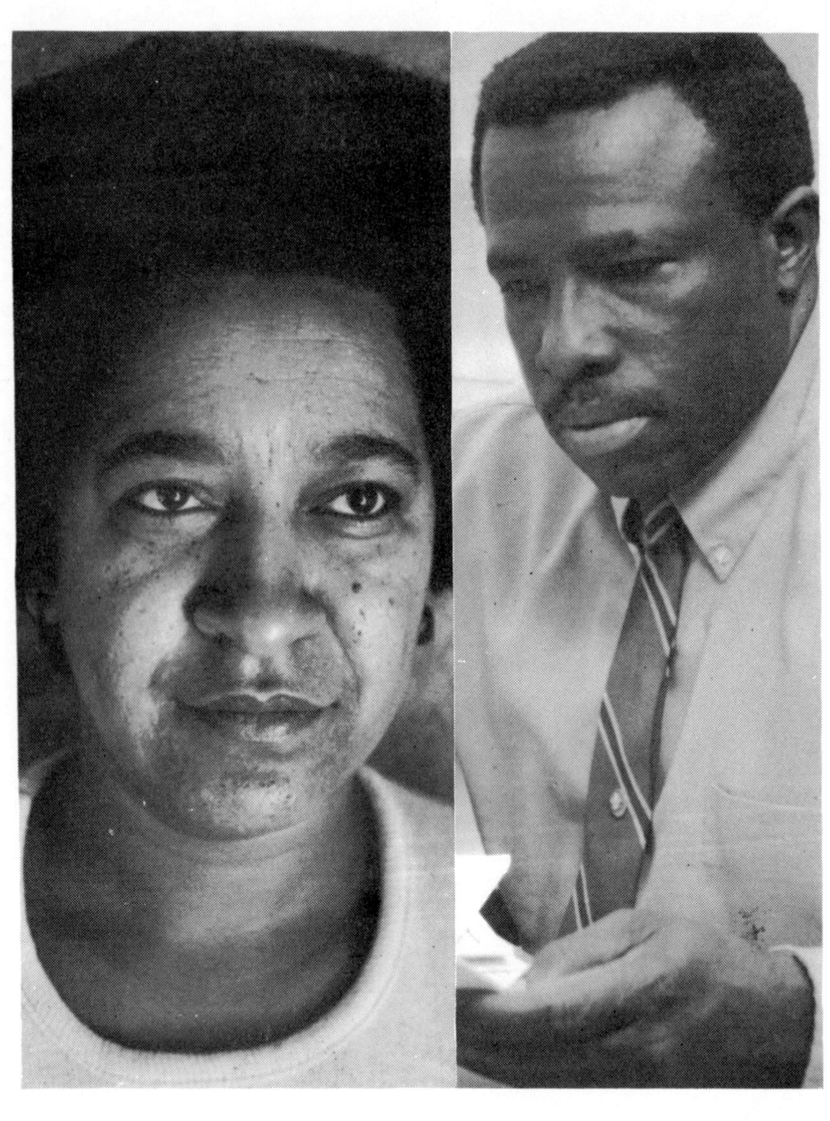

Restitution Fund Commission members: left to right: Mrs. Dolores E. Dow, and Dr. Herbert I. James.

Restitution Fund Commission members:
The Reverends Oscar E. Holder and John R. Logan.

The establishment. . . .

The special convention of the Diocese of Pennsylvania which met on May 23, 1970, to consider the report and final recommendations of the Task Force for Reconciliation passed a resolution which provided for:

> the establishment of an *Episcopal Restitution* Fund for black self-determination projects and the establishment of a *Restitution Fund Commission* composed of black Episcopalians (clergy and lay) to administer the Fund in keeping with the principles of self-determination.

The details, stipulated in the Task Force recommendations, included the following:

1. *Commission Membership* shall consist of:
   a. all black clergy of the Diocese, plus
   b. an equal number of lay persons (except only the provision for youth).

2. *Method of Selection:* Episcopalians shall be members on the basis of being:
   a. Black clergy, active in parochial, retired or any other official capacity in the Diocese.
   b. Black lay persons shall be members upon appointment by vestries, one from each predominantly black Protestant Episcopal Church in the Diocese. For this purpose, such a church shall be defined as a Protestant Episcopal Congregation with 90% or more black communicants, in addition to a black priest.

3. To insure that every black Episcopalian in the Diocese is given the opportunity to be considered for selection to the Commission, each church in the Diocese having no representatives selected under item "b" above, shall be invited to nominate, through its vestry, a black lay communicant of that church for consideration for membership on the Commission.

4. Persons selected under item "b" above shall constitute themselves as a committee and shall meet on a pre-determined date, before any meeting of the entire committee, for the purpose of selecting from the nominees called for in "3" above, a sufficient number of lay persons to make a total equal to the number of clergy on the Commission.

5. In the event that through the process outlined above that there do not appear on the Commission at least two (2) persons under 21 years of age, the Commission as a whole shall elect according to its own agreed-upon design, as many as two (2) black youths of less than 21 years of age to assure that they are represented on the Commission at least to the extent of two (2) members.

Clergy in the Diocese were notified of their selection to membership on the Commission. Predominantly black Protestant Episcopal churches in the Diocese were requested to select one lay person each as members of the Commission. All other parishes in the Diocese were given information on the establishment of the Commission and requested to nominate, through their vestries, a black lay communicant, if available, for consideration for membership on the Commission.

With the able assistance of the Reverend James Blackburn, Coordinator of the Episcopal Reconciliation Program, the first phase of this work was completed. In early June, 1970, eight of the ten laymen who had been selected from Black churches for membership on the Commission met at St. Philip's Church on Lombard Street in Philadelphia for the purpose of electing nine lay members from nominations of black members, who had been submitted from 15 other parishes in the Diocese. The nine laymen were elected. It was decided that the election of two youth members would be left to the Commission for consideration at its first meeting.

The task of the notification and assembling of clergy and lay members for the Commission fell upon the Very Reverend Kenneth O. Grannum and Alfred T. Dorsey, members of the Task Force for Reconciliation who had been designated as co-conveners.

The co-conveners called the first meeting of the full Commission for June 25, 1970. Telegrams were sent to all members of the Commission announcing such a meeting.

The complete list of those chosen for membership on the Commission and invited to its first meeting follows:

1. The Rev. Jesse F. Anderson, St. Thomas', West Philadelphia
2. Mr. John Bamber, Christ Church—St. Michael's, Germantown
3. Mrs. Nellie A. Barnes, St. Philip's, Philadelphia
4. Mr. Lawrence Barron, St. Mary's, Philadelphia
5. The Rev. Van S. Bird, St. Bartholomew's, Shibe Park
6. Mr. James Blake, St. Dunston Church, Blue Bell
7. The Rev. Matthew W. Davis, St. Andrew's and St. Monica, Philadelphia
8. Mrs. Dolores E. Dow, Calvary Church, Germantown
9. The Rev. Robert E. DuBose, Jr., House of Prayer, Philadelphia
10. Mr. Lawrence Fisher, Church of the Annunciation, Philadelphia

11. Mr. Paul Gibson, Church of the Redemption, Southampton
12. The Rev. Peter Golden, St. Augustine's Church, Philadelphia
13. The Rev. Kenneth O. Grannum, St. Philip's Memorial, Philadelphia
14. The Rev. Robert S. Harris, Church of the Annunciation, Philadelphia
15. The Rev. Richard Hicks, Jr., Non-Parochial; Campus Minister to Lincoln Univ. and Cheyney State College
16. The Rev. Oscar E. Holder, Memorial Chapel of the Holy Communion, Philadelphia
17. Mrs. Edith Huggins, Trinity Memorial Church, Philadelphia
18. Dr. Herbert James, St. Paul's Church, Levittown
19. The Rev. William G. Johnson, St. Andrew's and St. Monica, Philadelphia
20. The Rev. John R. Logan, Jr., St. Simon the Cyrenian, Philadelphia
21. The Very Rev. Thomas W. S. Logan, Calvary, Northern Liberties, Philadelphia
22. The Rev. Donald E. Lowry, Trinity Church, Swarthmore
23. The Rev. William Maddox, St. Mary's, Chester
24. Mr. Harold May, Trinity Church, Gulph Mills
25. Mr. Lances McKnight, Jr., Christ Church, Media
26. The Rev. Arthur C. Moore, St. Luke's, Germantown
27. Mrs. Sadie Mitchell, St. Thomas', Philadelphia
28. Mr. Harold E. Pilgrim, Calvary, Northern Liberties, Philadelphia
29. The Rev. Charles L. Poindexter, St. Luke's, Germantown
30. Dr. Walter N. Ridley, Church of the Holy Trinity, West Chester
31. Mr. James Robinson, House of Prayer, Philadelphia
32. Mr. William Rowe, St. Bartholomew's, Shibe Park
33. Mr. William Scott, St. Luke's, Germantown
34. Mr. Arthur Slater, St. Augustine's Church of the Covenant, Philadelphia
35. The Rev. William D. Turner, St. Augustine's Church of the Convenant, Philadelphia
36. The Rev. Paul M. Washington, Church of the Advocate, Philadelphia
37. The Rev. Wilson H. Williard, Jr., St. Mary's, Wayne
38. The Rev. Bruce P. Williamson, St. Mary's, Philadelphia
39. Mr. Theodore Wing, St. Simon's the Cyrenian, Philadelphia
40. The Rev. James E. P. Woodruff, Non-Parochial; Executive Director, Union of Black Clergy and Laity

The forty Episcopalians listed constituted the original membership of the Restitution Fund Commission of the Episcopal Diocese of Pennsylvania. They were composed of 21 black clergymen and 19 laymen. Soon to be added to the Commission were five other persons—one clergy and four lay. Mrs. Barbara Harris was named as the representative of the Church of the Advocate. Edward Bell was named to represent St. Andrew's and St. Monica's. Miss Pamela Horn and Greg Robinson were named as youth representatives. The Reverend Richard C. Winn later came to the Diocese and, as Vicar of St. Augustine's, Norristown, became a member of the Commission.

Thus, the Commission early listed among its membership 22 clergymen and 23 lay persons—a total of 45 persons named to the Commission. Six never became active. These included five laymen (Bell, Fisher, Horn, Huggins, and Wing), and one clergyman (Lowry). Most of these latter individuals never attended a meeting of the Commission. One attended only one meeting.

Two other laymen were members of the Commission at considerably later dates. Charles W. Polk was appointed as a replacement representative of St. Andrew's and St. Monica and Mrs. Lillian Booker was appointed as replacement to represent St. Simon the Cyrenian. These additions did not increase the total membership of the Commission since six appointees never responded positively to the invitation to contribute to the work of the Commission and some appointments were delayed. The active membership of the Commission never numbered more than thirty-nine persons.

The first meeting of the newly-constituted Restitution Fund Commission of the Episcopal Diocese of Pennsylvania was held on June 29, 1970, at the St. Philip's Episcopal Church on Lombard Street in Philadelphia. The Rev. Kenneth Grannum presided. The business included first a report on the method of selecting membership and constituency, and the functions of the committee. A question was raised whether the Commission should wait until the appointment of the two youth representatives before the selection of officers. A final decision was made to select officers pro-tem. Nominations were made and the following officers were elected:

1. Mr. Harold Pilgrim, Chairman
2. Dr. Walter N. Ridley, Vice Chairman
3. Mrs. Nellie A. Barnes, Secretary

4. Father William D. Turner, Treasurer

At this first meeting, Father Grannum reported that $8,599 in cash was at the disposal of the Commission. Dr. Ridley reported that members of the Task Force on Reconciliation had pledged $25,000 toward the Restitution Fund. It was agreed that an executive committee would be composed of the officers of the Commission, and that the Chairman might invite other persons to meet with the executive committee.

The first meeting of the executive committee was held on July 6, 1970. At this meeting it was suggested that five committees be appointed to do the ground work in several areas and to make recommendations to the Commission. The following committees were established with the understanding that each chairman had the authority to select members of the Commission to work on his/her committee:

1. Constitution and By-Laws: Dr. Walter N. Ridley, Chairman
2. Contacts and Public Relations: Rev. Kenneth Grannum, Chairman
3. Evaluation and Adjustments: Mrs. Sadie Mitchell, Chairman
4. Plans, Projects and Priorities: William Scott, Chairman
5. Reports and Information: Rev. Thomas Logan, Chairman

The Executive Committee planned an agenda for monthly meetings and directed that proper notice be given to Church House of the name of our treasurer with a request that funds be forwarded to the Commission. The treasurer was to be bonded for $50,000. It was agreed that vouchers for payments should bear the signature of the Chairman and Secretary, and checks would be signed by the Treasurer.

The second meeting of the Commission was held on July 28, 1970. A first check for funds had been received from the Church House. The five committees suggested by the executive committee made reports. There were additional suggestions that a historian be appointed, and that a central office for our activities be selected. The Rev. Mr. Davis of St. Andrew's and St. Monica offered office space for the work of the Commission in that church property. A committee was appointed to look into this matter. It was at this meeting that the youth representatives, Pamela Horn and Greg Robinson, were elected by the Commission. Suggestions were made regarding the deposit of funds.

By the third meeting, August 25, 1970, the inactivity of some of the members was noted and the chairman directed that the Committee on Contacts and Public Relations keep a record of membership participation and be responsible for replacements. The Chairman reported a telephone call received from Muhammad Kenyatta requesting to meet with members of the Commission during the first week in September. Members of the Commission felt that it would be premature to have visits from non-members during this period while the Commission itself was trying to move toward designing and effecting its own work.

At this meeting the Commission decided to place a major portion of the funds received in interest accounts in order to add to the funds. It was felt that the members of the Commission needed to spend an extended time together other than at regular meetings, to know each other better. A committee for this purpose was appointed. The Committee on Plans, Projects and Priorities reported having received some applications for funds.

By the time of the fourth meeting held at St. Simon the Cyrenian on September 22, 1970, the Commission had received more than $17,000.00 from the Diocese. The hope was expressed by the Treasurer of the Diocese that an amount of approximately $230,000 additional would be released in the very near future.

The question was raised at this meeting whether the Commission had any obligation or intention to make reports to the Diocese or to members of the Diocese. The Commission accepted the office space offered by St. Andrew's and St. Monica Church, and gave authority to the Executive Committee to spend a reasonable amount of money furnishing the office space. The Chairman reported that he had been contacted again by Mr. Kenyatta, who requested that he be notified "when the $500,000 check from the Diocese was received." Father Oscar Holder was appointed parliamentarian for the Commission.

The establishment of the Commission and its activities during the first four meetings is a record of the decisions. Almost every action of the Commission was accomplished after considerable discussion and with varied objection, some rather severe.

This development of the Restitution Commission's operational regulation and schedule took time, and the clamor for action grew. In the face of dire need which existed, some thought, delay was intolerable.

We move next to a crucial confrontation over these differences in approach.

Chapter XI

The Reverend Paul Washington.

The Reverend Kenneth Grannum.

From policy to process. . . .

The general policies and directions for the Restitution Fund Commission emerged. This was provided by the votes for approval of the large majority of the members at the first five commission sessions. With this favorable nod, the process began.

The major committees, which had been established during the first and second meetings of the Restitution Commission and the Executive Council became the nuclei from which emanated the real work of the Commission. Each committee made recommendations to the Commission. These activities for policy personnel and action greatly facilitated the work.

All of the Committees were counted important and so regarded, but in these beginning days of the Commission, the Executive Committee and the Committees on Constitution and By-Laws, and on Plans, Projects and Priorities found their efforts of extreme importance for getting the Commission "off the ground."

The Executive Committee, composed of the officers of the Commission, plus two elected members, with Harold Pilgrim as its chairman, sifted through inquiries, recommendations and policies. These findings were shared, and these specific recommendations made the full Commission much more effective.

The Committee on Constitution and By-Laws was organized in the second (July, 1970) meeting of the Commission. Dr. Walter N. Ridley was named its chairman. It sought and received input from members of the Commission, considered principles of organizational structure, held many meetings, and made several presentations to the group. The Constitution was provisionally accepted by the Commission in the sixth (November, 1970) meeting. The By-laws were also presented in the sixth meeting. However, the Constitution and the By-laws were both finally adopted after revisions and adjustments in the seventh (December, 1970) and the ninth (February, 1971) meetings, respectively.

The Committee on Plans and Projects, chaired by William A. Scott, decided that its first assignment would be an agreement on the types of grants to be considered, levels of priorities to be assigned to the various applications, projects and programs and determination of its own operational plans.

Members of this committee met many hours in order to answer such questions as: "What is the meaning of black self-determination projects?", "What processes should be employed in the collection of data regarding applicants?", "Can the committee members do such investigating and evaluation as required or do we need outside investigative personnel?", "What relative weight should be given to the priorities of the community, of the Commission, of the Church?"

The P.P.P. Committee (as it was commonly called) received applications from individuals and agencies. P.P.P. found as time passed that inquiries and pressures from applicants and sponsors increased dramatically.

The Committee on Reports and Information, with the Rev. Thomas S. Logan as its chairman, studied the Community and the Committee contributions. These research and production recommendation reports served the interest of both community and Commission. This committee did not issue any such formal reports. However, from time to time constructive oral statements and suggestions were made by the chairman.

The Committee on Contact and Public Relations with the Rev. Kenneth O. Grannum as its chairman made efforts from the beginning to collect information from committees and members, and to study and collate these into public relations pieces. From time to time, and especially for the Diocesan conventions, the Restitution Commission produced comprehensive summaries on the policies, on grants made, or on the educational grants made to students. Displays and bulletin boards were utilized in order to interpret the Commission and its work to the members of the Diocese.

The Committee on Evaluation and Adjustments, with Mrs. Sadie Mitchell as its chairman, assessed and made recommendations regarding the work of the Commission and its committees, toward the goals of the coordination of efforts and the smooth, efficient operation of the whole Commission. This Committee early studied the operations of the various elements in the Commission and made constructive suggestions, time requirements, and interpretative statements which proved of value. Although some individuals and committees seemed to feel that the work of this committee was a threat to their independence, the Committee continued its work diligently and the Commission as a whole, and the processes in which it was engaged profited from the efforts of the Committee on Evaluation and Adjustments. Several other ad hoc committees were appointed from time to time, but six committees, plus the Education Committee later appointed, remained the long-term contributors to the overall work of the Commission. . . and yet, it must be said in fairness to all concerned that all of these committees and the Commission as a whole, were victimized by the inherent inadequacies and difficulties which come with a volunteer system such as that upon which the Commission depended for the major part of its work.

The Restitution Fund Commission never obtained any paid services except those of part-time employees, and this was done intermittently and constituted a minor portion of the work done over the six-year period from 1970. All of the background thought, organization, planning, refinement, leg work, and production of philosophy, policies and process were done by contributing members of the Commission. The members did seventy-five percent of the investigating and all of the interpretation and recommendation regarding grants. They produced the application form and did the processing for all of the educational and for three-fourths of the other applications for grants. These members added this work to already busy personal schedules of full-time employment and, for the majority, considerable involved commitment to several other church or community activities or projects. The average active members contributed hundreds of hours to this work. Some persons, who have been consistent in their contributions over the six-year period, contributed thousands of hours of travel, study, and work to the Commission. These efforts were without remuneration or reimbursement.

Chapter XII

A Station Wagon Financed by RFC Can Be A Real Help.

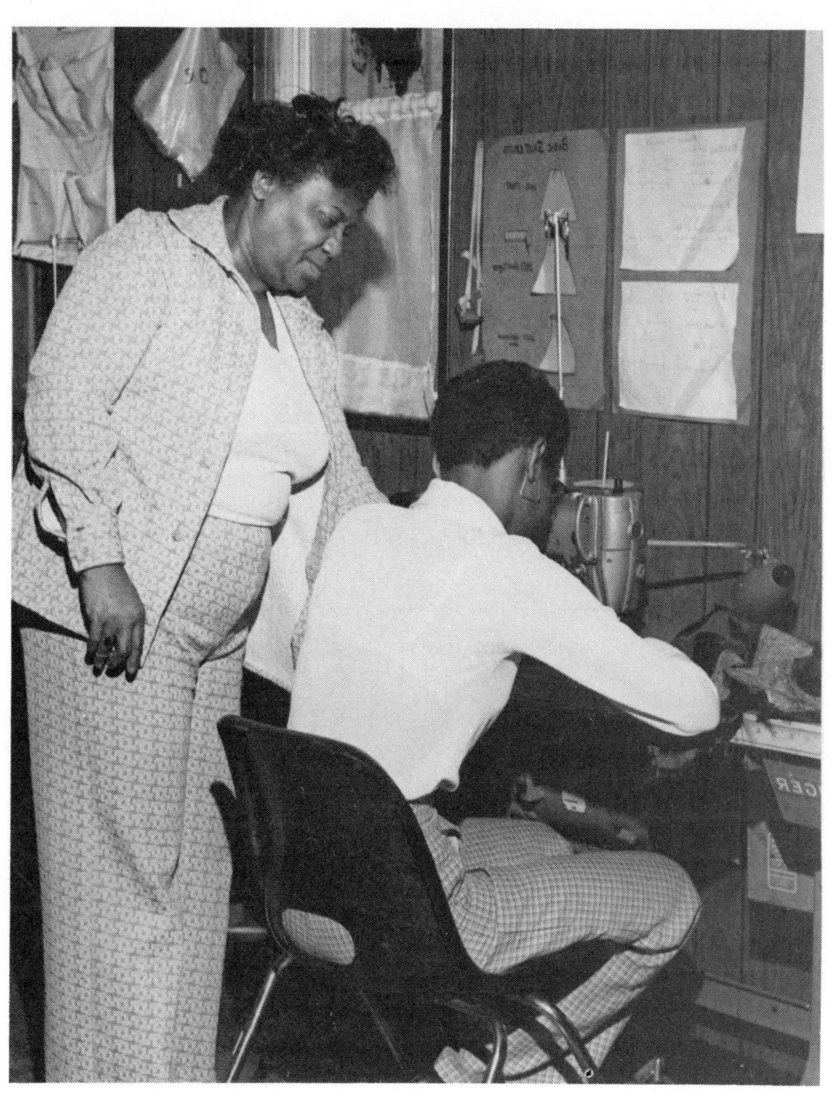

Ms. Lillian H. Randolph, Sewing Instructor,
and student; Lorraine Huff.

Diversities and Dichotomies.

At the first full meeting of the Restitution Fund Commission held at St. Philip's Church on June 29, 1970, after the opening prayers by Father Arthur C. Moore and the reading of the minutes of the meeting on the selection of the final group of lay members to be added, the floor was declared open for business. It was immediately evident, upon the suggestion that there be the election of officers, that, at least among those who were outspoken, there was not so much a divergence of opinions and points of view centered around a common midpoint but a wider-than-expected divergence of points of view which constituted more of a dichotomy than a difference.

The members of the Commission showed deep and thoughtful concern regarding the philosophy, organization, and functioning of the Commission. They were serious and addressed themselves to the business at hand. However, this first and the three succeeding meetings of the Commission revealed a remarkable soul-searching. These meetings were filled with statements of convictions regarding the various interpretations of the mission, the procedures, and the responsibilities of the Commission. Some of the areas which took much time and animated discussion during these four meetings centered around the following:

1. Shall we organize the Commission tc function as a structured body, on the basis of generally accepted practices of parliamentary order? Or, should we refrain from organizing and function as a consensus-seeking group, more like a "tribal council"? Do we need parliamentary formality? Can we not move by consensus and the expressed desires of the group without the formality of motions, voting, etc.? Do we need a permanent structure now? Do we need an executive and other committees to sift through the problems and to come to the Commission with substantive suggestions for final decisions? Cannot the entire body meet, hear all of the business, and attend to it?
2. Shall the leadership of the Commission be clergy or lay? Shall they be "organization-minded" or "free-flowing consensus-minded" persons? Can our leadership be "diocese-oriented" and, at the same time, administer to the needs of the black community?
3. Are we not a self-determined body to the extent of having no need to communicate to the Diocese or to the public any information relative to finances received and expended, projects funded, and progress in the work of the Commission? Have we a responsibility to Episcopalians of the Diocese to keep them informed of the work of the Commission?
4. Is not five million dollars assured the Commission within a period

of a very few years? Has the half million dollars, which was to be given immediately, arrived? Are these reasonable expectations?

5. Should there be established philosophy, guidelines, and procedures before grants are made on individual merits without reference to the needs of the whole community? Should any monies received be granted to community groups making applications as soon as requests are made, and based upon statements of need? Do we need to investigate stated needs?
6. Should we give preference to high-risk new community organizations, not necessarily conventional in their purposes or designs, which do not have access to the regular sources of funding available in the community? Should we be slow to fund unproven high-risk projects?
7. Should we make grants immediately to black Episcopal churches with tight budgets in order to help satisfy their capital and program needs? Or should we make grants only to projects providing other than religious services for well-being of needful persons in the community?

The first of several meetings of the Restitution Fund Commission wrestled nightly with these problems. Though, at times, seemingly slow and laborious, the process was pursued with diligence. The process centered around beliefs and convictions, for, although each "side" defended its positions vigorously and ardently, personal animosities and references were minimal despite the heat of the debate. Finally, agreements were made by majority vote on the direction which the Commission would take. The major early decisions of the Commission evidenced by the end of the fourth meeting included the following:

1. That the Commission be organized and its functions should be based upon regularly accepted procedures.
2. That adequate space and office and communications equipment should be obtained to house the work and functions of the Commission.
3. That all funds received by the Commission be handled in a proper and responsible manner by duly-elected officers of the Commission, under bond. Also, that whereas enough funds to assure a cash flow sufficient to take care of needs should be maintained in checking account, any funds received above this need should be placed in interest-bearing accounts, available on short notice of need.
4. That since the business brought to the Commission would require its whole attention and work, there would be only a minimum of appearances by any non-members before the Commission as a whole.

5. That all grants, after study and investigation, be made only upon the action of the whole Commission in a regularly-called meeting.
6. That there be a historical record of the Commission and its work.
7. That all applications made be processed and investigated, and recommendations for grants made on a system of priorities—that a system of priorities would be established and all projects brought before the Commission would be brought after investigation and recommendation by the Committee on Plans, Projects, and Priorities.
8. That a constitution and by-laws for the Commission be developed. A committee for this purpose was created.
9. That there be contacts and public relations pursued to keep the work of the Commission before the parishioners in the Diocese and the public. A Committee on Contacts and Public Relations was formed.
10. That the reports, business, and information coming to the Commission be organized, codified and made available for use of the Commission. A Committee on Reports and Information was authorized.
11. That the organization functioning and all work of the Commission be subject to evaluation and suggestions for adjustments in order to maintain effectiveness and efficiency. A Committee on Evaluation and Adjustment was formed.
12. That the Executive and other committees follow the approved and organized arrangement for the transaction of the business of the Commission, and make reports to the regular meetings of the Commission.
13. That high-risk as well as stabilized community organizations and agencies be considered for grants from the Commission.
14. That the Commission not grant funds to support the religious programs or capital needs of black Episcopal churches, but that projects which provide other than religious services would be considered regardless of their church affiliations.

Thrashing out and forging of the policies and procedures were the major activities of the Commission during the first four meetings. By the fifth meeting held in November of 1970, the total receipts of the Commission from the Diocese had amounted to $98,573.04. At the November meeting, the by-laws for the Commission were accepted provisionally, after reading suggestions and corrections, which were to be inserted. The constitution was presented also for the first time at this meeting.

A report from the Committee on Plans, Projects, and Priorities was made and accepted. Questions were raised at this meeting with regard to emergency funding. The chairman reported that one project for emergency funding was being considered. However, some members felt that emergencies should be handled in the meetings directly, rather than through the committees.

Chapter XIII

Chairman Harold Pilgrim of The Restitution Fund Commission.

Friends of St. John's Settlement House receive citations.

*. . . Confrontation—Disruption—
Departure. . .*

As with most human organizations, RFC suffered from some elements in its fabric. These included (1) the length of time taken (or required) for the conversion of policies and ideas into processes and actions, especially when dependent upon a volunteer system, (2) the necessity of being responsive to the community and to the designs, attitudes, and wishes of several populations—some to the left and some to the right, (3) the unsettling effects of the planned actions of individuals or groups who felt sincerely that the Commission needed "shock treatment" or attack in order for it to be moved in directions which these individuals desired or, indeed, perhaps, to move at all, and (4) the election of lay leadership in the Commission, which was originally suggested to be composed completely of members of the clergy.

There were three episodes during the first year in the life of the Commission which were interpreted, in the minds of some persons, to represent the general nature of the Commission and its existence and functioning. Some other persons, including the majority of the members of the Commission, interpreted these to represent episodes and obstacles to be dealt with as occurances, perhaps unfortunate, to be overcome, but neither deterring, nor defeating in the life and work of the Commission.

"Critical" and "decisive" are words which describe the fifth meeting of the Commission. At this meeting held on October 27, 1970, at St. Luke's Church, Germantown, the divergencies which had been evidenced in previous meetings by some of the members erupted into open confrontation. Before the roll call could be accomplished, the Reverend Wilson H. Williard of St. Mary's Church, Wayne, insisted on offering a motion. The motion read, "to suspend the regular agenda, go into a committee of the whole, and appoint Mrs. Saddie Mitchell as chairman for said committee." The structure of the motion having been questioned by the chairman and others, the motion was not sustained in an appeal vote. A later motion by Fathers Woodruff and Maddox, "to go into a committee of the whole" was passed. Dr. Ridley was selected as chairman of the committee and for an hour and a half, beginning with fulminations from both sides, there was a venting of ideas, interrogatives, concerns, and challenges.

The content of this "committee discussion" centered around the ideas previously listed as divergencies. Reference was made that the Hawkins Report recommended that the Commission membership consist entirely of black clergy, but that this idea had given way to the inclusion of an equal number of lay persons. There were attacks upon the chairman, officers, and committees. There was an attempt to differentiate among the lay membership on the basis of their having come from "black churches" and "white churches." There were efforts to move into immediate funding of requests on the basis of applications without investigation and based on their classification as emergencies. When brought to votes, however, none of these ideas prevailed.

It was at the crucial fifth meeting that the general nature of the Commission and its procedures and work were critically tested by some members who disagreed especially with the procedures. This eventual "fifth" which might have been expected to have terminated in a fracture in the Commission, appeared to end in a more common understanding of the purposes of the Commission among the members, who remained. Although all did not agree on procedures, the purposes emerged a commonality, and neither the purposes nor procedures were changed. The chairman, officers, committees, and the Commission after this disharmony, moved more determinedly about the work.

The demand that the money be turned over to a militant source persisted. On October 21, 1971, about 25 persons from five black organizations launched a campaign to force the head of the Episcopal Church's Restitution Fund Commission to act on their groups' requests for funds.

After a two-hour meeting in the West Philadelphia office of Harold L. Pilgrim, chairman of the Commission, some of the dissidents launched a sit-in; others began following Pilgrim when he left the office.

They complained that Mr. Pilgrim and the 40-member commission of black laymen and clergy have been slow in distributing money to worthy black organizations and had failed to respond.

Led by Muhammad Kenyatta, Chairman of the Black Economic Development Conference, the groups charged that the Commission had given out only $32,000 of the $500,000 in the church's Restitution Fund money earmarked for black-owned businesses and programs.

Demanding that he resign, the demonstrators accused Mr. Pilgrim of "standing in the way of black progress." Pilgrim said he would not resign and told the group he was "powerless" to respond alone to their requests.

After the dialogue, Mr. Pilgrim left the office at 1304 N. 52nd Street, followed by about half the demonstrators who said they were determined to remain with him until after the church's annual Diocesan Convention which began that afternoon. Mr. Pilgrim was to report for the convention at 4:00 p.m. The remainder announced they would sit in Mr. Pilgrim's office.

The black groups were House Umoja, Concerned Tradesmen, Mantua Community Employment Service, Evangelist Summer Project and BEDC.

These words, uttered under dramatic circumstances and poignant times, were to set a climate in which the Restitution Fund Commission was to operate: "As soon as you get the $500,000, let me know."

The third such episode might well be called the "Exodus." The Very Rev. Thomas Logan had suggested that for the June 1971 meeting of the Commission RFC "celebrate its first anniversary" in a religious service to which the Bishop would be invited. RFC would install officers and hold the service at St. Philip's Church, where the first meeting was held. Father Logan was appointed chairman to work with Fathers Poindexter and Grannum in arranging for this function. He reported that the Bishop had accepted the invitation to give the absolution and benediction as well as to install the officers. Dr. Ridley was requested to review the purposes of the Commission and its functioning to date, and Father Paul Washington was asked to give the sermon.

The time arrived and with Father Grannum presiding, the services commenced. Father Grannum's introductory welcoming statements were interrupted by Muhammad Kenyatta, who suggested that he represented the poor and the needy people who were not being served by the Commission. "The Commission must move to assuage the needs of the people," he said. Dr. Ridley reviewed the purposes, organization and work of the Commission to date. Father Washington started his sermon and in it he voiced severe unrest and dissatisfaction on the part of some members of the Commission with the way in which the Commission and its work had been going. He castigated the officers and members for allowing many policies to delay the immediate distribution of funds while there were so many persons "around us" suffering and in dire need. In his brief, emotion-charged, caustic and pungent statement, using, at times, what is politely called "street language," he declared that he and some other members would leave the Commission in protest.

Bishop DeWitt pronounced the benediction. He made no references to the strange occurrences of the evening. He left immediately after the service, not remaining for the brief social hour that had been arranged. Some members expressed surprise and disappointment that the Bishop had failed to call attention to what many thought was a misuse of the pulpit in the sermon, or at least to make a "healing statement" in the face of the impending schism in the Commission.

The "chatter and prattle" which erupted from this episode, especially in church circles, were remarkable. They ranged from "there is a minor fracture in the Commission," to "the Commission is broken up and deserted." Perhaps the most damaging effects of the schism were (1) a definite loss of a third of the Commission manpower and their sharing the constructive work yet to be done in the realization of the goals of the Commission, and (2) the provision of a quickly exploited excuse for a number of members of the Diocese, who had never supported or really wanted the Commission, to label it as "ineffective, unneeded, and worthy of desertion." Actually, fourteen of the thirty-nine members listed on the Commission at this time departed at this point. Departing were four laymen and ten priests. Seventy-nine percent of the laymen and fifty percent of the clergymen who were members of the Commission did not depart. Thus, sixty-five percent of the whole membership was left to carry on the work. Those who departed were Ms. Barbara Harris, Ms. Sadie Mitchell, James Robinson, William Rowe, and the Reverends Jessie Anderson, Van Bird, Robert DuBose, Peter Golden, Richard Hicks, Arthur Moore, Paul Washington, Wilson Williard, Richard Wynn and James Woodruff.

The persons who departed the Commission constituted the principal, active membership of the Union of Black Clergy and Laity. The departure of these important persons took its toll, but this made those who remained even more careful and determined to proceed with care and caution and effectiveness.

Chapter XIV

A Clean-up Detail.

Pride in Achievement at an RFC Supported Child Care Center.

The operational philosophy. . . .

A true operating philosophy is more than words reduced to paper, it is a "feeling of the heart." Likewise, establishment of levels of priorities is an arbitrary venture supported by exigencies of the time and experience of personalities. The priorities, when written, provide a substantive base of discussion and decision.

There were those who contend that "spending of money for the Restitution should not be closely surrounded with rules and regulations. These individuals, honest and concerned persons, believed that the "needs of the moment" transcended "sanguinity of action."

Suffice to say, the guidelines which the Restitution Committee established provided a base of operation. Because these determinants "speak eloquently for themselves," we present them here.

THE OPERATING PHILOSOPHY AND LEVELS OF PRIORITIES FOR THE RESTITUTION FUND COMMISSION, DIOCESE OF PENNSYLVANIA

Part I—Philosophy

GUIDELINES FOR APPLICATIONS

I. Purposes:

The application shall fall into one or more of these three categories:

A. Black self-determination on a metropolitan and or neighborhood level for social, political or economic power including basic research and planning to these ends.

B. Programs of service to the Black community designed and controlled by those to be served.

C. Community leadership training and experience in areas of need identified by the applicants.

II. Criteria:

A. In conformity to the Constitution and By-Laws of the Restitution Fund Commission:

1. The purpose and ends sought to be obtained by the proposed program fall within one or more of the Purposes enumerated above.
2. The proposed program is based upon the fundamental principle of Black self-determination.
3. The proposed program, by its terms, provides that neither the Diocese of Pennsylvania or the Diocesan Council, nor any officer thereof, shall exercise any supervision or control whatsoever over:

a. the proposed grant, or

b. the administration and execution thereof by the recipient, or

c. the ends and purposes sought to be obtained thereby

4. The proposed program, by its terms, provides for a periodical review with the administration of the organization being funded.

The Committee on Plans, Projects and Priorities in its evaluations shall determine, as a part of its initial appraisal of the proposed programs, that the proposed grant recipient is reasonably able to attain the purposes and ends sought thereby.

B. Need:

1. Is there a valid local or metropolitan need for this project?
2. How is this need demonstrated? Statistics, personal testimony, other?

C. Feasibility:

1. Do the stated purposes, objectives and timetable represent a coherent, reasonable plan?
2. Will this project have a wide range of impact on society?
3. Is there a high degree of readiness for the project? (actors, sponsors, system)
4. Can the project accomplish its goals without an unhealthy dependence on other agencies?
5. Is the project non-paternalistic?
6. Does the proposed promise increased self-determination for Black people?

D. Use of Resources:

1. Is the budget realistic?
2. Are there budget projections for eventual self-support?
3. Will this project generate other sources of funding if the Restitution Fund Commission supports it?
4. Are the required trained personnel available and ready?
5. Is there a reasonable plan for human resources development?

E. Local Support:

1. Who wants this project?
2. Can the proponents demonstrate a significant base of support for initiating or continuing this project?
3. Have the constituency participated in the planning and designing of the program or is it just the work of professionals?
4. What is the overall relationship between this program and the members of the neighborhood or community?

Part II—Mechanics

I. Rationale:

A. The following levels of Priorities are based on the philosophy outlined in Part I.

B. Proposals at a specific level may not be funded until all other proposals of higher level (numerically lower) have been acted upon; i.e., investigated, recommendations submitted, and appropriate action taken by the Commission. Periodic evaluation for the reassignment of project levels on hand will be made every three months.

C. Applications or proposals may not be funded prior to a review, investigation and recommendations by the Committee on Plans, Projects and Priorities.

Level I—Those proposals conducive to Black self-determination which after investigation clearly indicate that a person's life or well-being or a group's existence is in jeopardy, after other avenues have been explored without necessary relief.

Level II—Any function or service performed by an organization that is:

a. conducive to Black self-determination.
b. needed by the community.
c. not presently performed by any other organization or individual in the community.
d. performed at a minimal or non-profit level to the recipient.
e. available at a maximum per capita for each dollar expended.

Level III—Any function or service performed by an organization that is:

a. conducive to Black self-determination.
b. needed by the community.
c. an expansion or refinement of service already performed by an organization or person in the community.
d. given at a minimal or non-profit level to the recipient.
e. available at a maximum per capita for each dollar expended.

Level IV—Any function or service performed by an organization that:

a. is conducive to Black self-determination.
b. is needed by the community.
c. is performed without regard for existing services which overlap or parallel.

d. may be performed at a favorable cost to the recipient.
e. may reach a restricted number of persons.

Level V—Any function or service performed by an organization that is:

a. conducive to Black self-determination.
b. needed by the community.
c. performed as may be expedient.
d. performed at a favorable cost to the recipient.
e. performed without regard to the number of persons involved.

Level VI—Any function or service performed by an organization or individual that has not been included in Level I through Level V above.

Chapter XV

In the Library, Institute of Black Ministers.

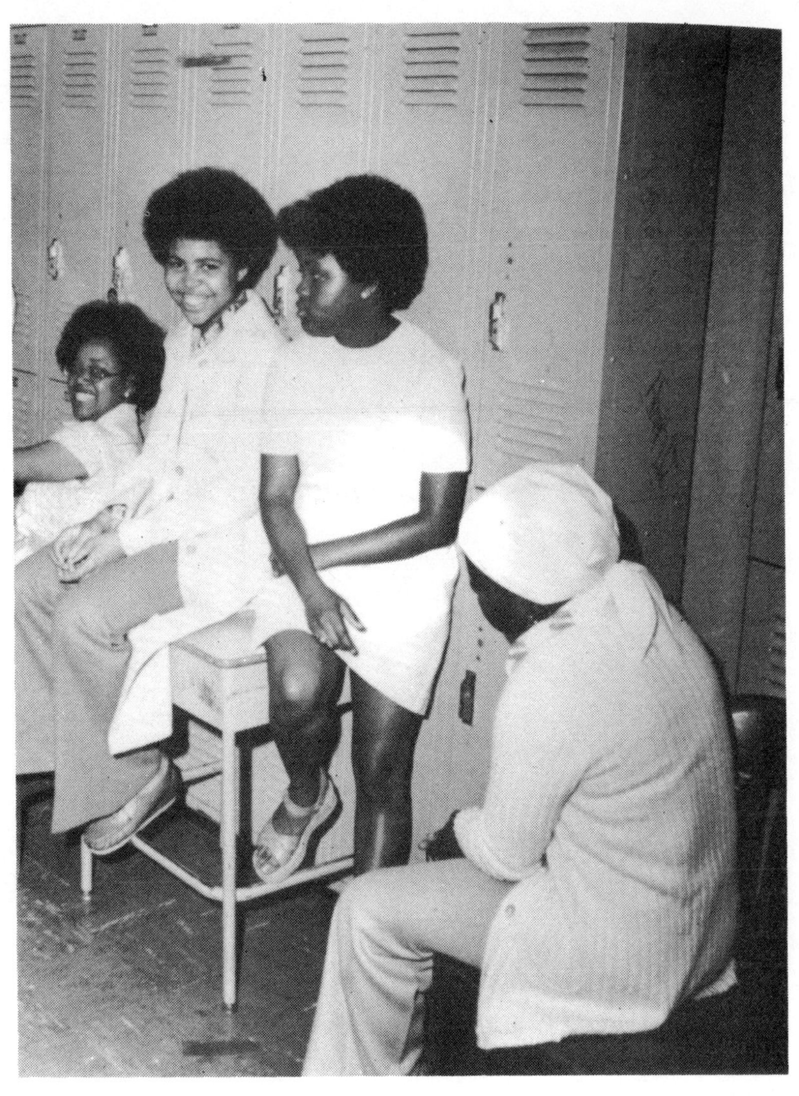

RFC support for Physical Education promotes confidence.

In Troubled Times For
Reconciliation In The Inner City

CONSTITUTION AND BY-LAWS

Restitution Fund Commission
Episcopal Diocese of Pennsylvania

Adoption
February 23, 1971

Amended
March 23, 1971

CONSTITUTION

ARTICLE I

Name

The name of this organization shall be THE RESTITUTION FUND COMMISSION, EPISCOPAL DIOCESE OF PENNSYLVANIA.

ARTICLE II

Purpose

The Restitution Fund Commission, as an entity within the Diocese of Pennsylvania, has as its purpose the location, development and sponsoring within and for the Black Community, of such programs and projects as arise from their self-determined aims and purposes and as will result in benefit to the community in the areas of its economic, political, educational and social well-being.

ARTICLE III

Locus And Nature

The Restitution Fund Commission shall be located within the Diocese of Pennsylvania. It shall be a non-profit incorporated body. Its work shall be principally within the Diocese of Pennsylvania.

ARTICLE IV

Membership

The membership of the Commission is set up by the TASK FORCE FOR RECONCILIATION FINAL RECOMMENDATIONS AND REPORT TO SPECIAL CONVENTION TOGETHER WITH THE ACTION OF SPECIAL CONVENTION of the Diocese of Pennsylvania, on May 23, 1970. This membership consists of Black

Clergy, active in parochial, retired or any other capacity in the Diocese, and Black Lay Persons upon appointment as described in the report. They should be in equal numbers, Clergy and Lay, except only in cases of provision for Youth Representatives as described. Retention and replacement of members shall be in accordance with By-Laws as adopted by the Restitution Fund Commission.

ARTICLE V

Annual Meeting

The Commission shall hold an annual meeting within the Diocese of Pennsylvania on the fourth Tuesday of each May, unless a different time is fixed on by a preceding annual meeting, or by a two-thirds vote of the Commission in a regular meeting.

ARTICLE VI

Officers

Officers of the Commission shall be a Chairman, a Vice-Chairman, a Recording Secretary, a Financial Secretary, and a Treasurer. These officers shall be elected according to dates set in the By-Laws of the Commission and shall take office at the first meeting after the beginning of the fiscal year of the Commission subsequent to their election. Their duties shall be those generally ascribed to such officers.

ARTICLE VII

Committees

There shall be an Executive Committee composed of the officers of the Commission plus four members elected from and by the Commission. Members of this Committee shall be elected at the same time as the officers. Functions of this Committee shall be those regularly given to such a committee except as voted specifically otherwise by the Commission.

ARTICLE VIII

Rules of Order

Proceedings of the Commission shall be conducted under and pursuant to Robert's Rules of Order, except as otherwise provided in the By-Laws. The President may or, when requested by the Commission, will appoint a Parliamentarian to function in the meetings of the Commission.

ARTICLE IX

Appeals

The right of appeal from any decision of the Commission, its officers and its committees is hereby established. An appeals Board shall be provided for in the By-Laws of the Commission, along with clear and functional procedures for the handling of appeals. The Commission itself is the final appeal authority. It shall assure that appeals are handled with efficiency, dispatch, fairness, openness and in line with the purpose of the Commission.

ARTICLE X

Finances

The Commission receives funds from the Diocese of Pennsylvania and other available sources. Such funds may be invested for periods of time while being held for us in furtherance of the purpose of the Commission. Handling of all funds shall be in line with general practices of fiscal and canonical responsibility.

ARTICLE XI

Amendments

This Constitution may be amended by a two-thirds vote at any regular meeting of the Commission, or special meeting called for the announced purposes of considering constitutional amendments, in the following manner:

1. The amendment shall be proposed in writing at a regular meeting and read for the information of the Commission.

2. The proposed amendment shall be duplicated and mailed to all members of the Commission at least fifteen days before the meeting in which it is to be voted upon, and

3. The date and time of the meeting in which the amendment is to be considered is included with the amendment when mailed to the members.

BY-LAWS

ARTICLE I

The Commission

A. The Commission year shall begin on July 1, and end on June 30, each year.

B. The Commission will meet at such time as it decides upon, provided, however, that there **must** be held at least one meeting in each quarter. The Chairman must convene a called meeting within ten days of receipt of a petition for same signed by at least ten of the members. The business to be transacted at such a meeting must be stated in the petition and in the notice for the meeting, and only such business as announced may be transacted.

C. Membership on the Commission involves responsibility to those whom one is selected to represent as well as to the entire community.

1. Membership on the Commission becomes official when the unit responsible for final selection or certification of members has communicated in writing with the Commission and announcement of same is made to the Commission.
2. If any member fails to attend three consecutive meetings of the Commission his/her vestry shall be informed of the fact, with the request that they take steps to secure more adequate representation through motivating the member or, in case of a lay member, submitting an alternate selection or nomination.
3. In case of acceptable excuses presented by the member, this action will be delayed but will ensue after the fourth absence.

D. A properly called meeting shall be in order and shall proceed with business at hand upon the presence of a presiding officer and a quorum, which shall be defined as one-third (⅓) of the membership (including officers).

ARTICLE II

Officers

A. Any member regular in attendance and in attention to the responsibilities assigned by the Commission shall be eligible for election to any office.

B. Officers of the Commission shall be (1) Chairman, (2) Vice-Chairman, (3) Recording Secretary, (4) Financial Secretary, and (5) Treasurer.

C. Duties of the officers shall be:

1. THE CHAIRMAN shall preside at all meetings of the Commission and of the Executive Committee. He shall appoint committees, have control of the official seal and be responsible for having it affixed to proper documents upon authorization of the Executive Committee. He shall have general responsibility for coordinating the work of all officers and committees and shall generally see that the policies and procedures agreed upon and/or designated by the Commission are properly carried into effect.
2. THE VICE CHAIRMAN, in the absence of the Chairman, shall preside at all meetings of the Commission and the Executive Committee. He shall serve as Chairman of the Committee on Appeals and shall perform such other duties as assigned by the Chairman or Commission.

   He shall be ex-officio a member of all standing committees and shall exercise such other powers and functions as are usually vested in the Chairman of a Commission, subject to the jurisdiction of the Commission.
3. THE RECORDING SECRETARY shall keep full minutes of all meetings of the Commission and the Executive Committee; shall record all votes; shall keep all of the proceedings in a permanent minute book of the Commission provided for this purpose; shall give notice of all meetings of the Commission and the Executive Committee; shall attest by signature the affixing of the seal of the Commission to authorize proper documents; and shall perform such other duties as prescribed by the Chairman.
4. THE FINANCIAL SECRETARY shall receive all funds of the Commission and maintain an accurate description

and record of all receipts and disbursements along with a record of actions of the Commission authorizing same. These shall be kept in a permanent record book of the Commission provided for that purpose. He shall render reports to the Chairman and Executive Committee at each regular meeting and to the Commission as required. He shall sign all vouchers found correct and proper for payment by the Treasurer and shall be bonded in such amount as required by the Executive Committee. He shall transfer all money items and cash received to the Treasurer and receive a receipt for same.

5. THE TREASURER shall receive all receipts from the Financial Secretary and shall issue to him a receipt for same. He shall deposit all monies and other valuable effects in the name and to the credit of the Commission in such depositories and accounts as are designated by the Executive Committee and approved by the Commission. He shall issue official numbered Commission checks for disbursement of Commission funds only upon receipt of properly executed vouchers signed by the Chairman and the Financial Secretary. He shall render to the Executive Committee and to the Commission at each regular meeting an account of the activity of his office and the financial condition of the Commission. He shall be bonded in such amount as set by the Executive Committee.

D. In case of extended absence of any officer or elected member of the Executive Committee, or for any other reason that the body deems sufficient, the Commission may delegate the duties or powers of such officers to any other officer or member of the Commission. This may be done by majority vote. Such action may be taken by the Executive Committee in any situation which it determines as demanding such action, provided, however, that such is subject to confirmation by the Commission at its next succeeding meeting. All this is subject to the requirement that anticipation of such action must be announced to all members eligible to participate in the meeting in which such action is to be considered at least seven (7) days prior to such meeting.

E. Vacancies in these offices shall be filled upon proper notification of the Commission and upon nomination and action as described in ARTICLE IV-B, at the next succeeding meeting of the Commission after such vacancy.

ARTICLE III

Committees

A. There shall be an EXECUTIVE COMMITTEE composed of the elected officers of the Commission plus four members elected by and from the Commission.

B. The Executive Committee shall be responsible for the proper operation of the business and affairs of the Commission and the adherence of all elements of the principles and policies established by the Commission. It shall consider and recommend to the Commission policies in pursuance of the purposes of the Commission. It shall be responsible for the preservation, conservation and proper use of any and all funds and properties of the Commission. It shall oversee the operation of the Commission including any employees. It shall hire and separate employees as authorized by the Commission.

C. The Executive Committee shall report its functions and recommendations to each meeting of the Commission. Actions of the Executive Committee are subject to the jurisdiction of the Commission. Actions recommended by the Committee may be sustained by a majority vote. The Executive Committee acts for the Commission as needed, while the Commission is not in session. Actions taken for the Commission shall require a two-thirds vote for reversal. Such reversal shall not create personal financial liability against any member of the Committee.

D. There shall be five STANDING COMMITTEES as follows:

1. PLANS, PROJECTS AND PRIORITIES—To receive, evaluate, plan and make recommendations on all applications for funding received.
2. CONSTITUTION AND BY-LAWS—to study the design, needs, policies and principles of the Commission and to recommend to it such constitutional and by-laws elements as will facilitate and or improve its being and operation.
3. REPORTS AND INFORMATION—to study the commu-

nity and the Commission and its work, and to prepare and issue from time to time such statistical and informational reports as will serve the interest of both.

4. CONTRACTS AND PUBLIC RELATIONS—to study the community and the Commission and its work, and to prepare official statements and reports for external and public consumption as will be in the interest of the community, and the work of the Commission. This committee shall act as the Commission's representatives to the news media.
5. EVALUATION AND ADJUSTMENTS—to evaluate periodically the functioning of the Commission and its subordinate bodies and to recommend, if necessary, what and when corrections may be needed to unify and make smooth the operation.

These committees may be assigned additional or different duties by the Chairman from time to time, and or he may recommend changes in their work to the Commission.

Membership on these committees should reflect well the overall nature of the Commission as well as the competencies of the Commission members in the work of the committees. Membership on each of these committees should be not less than five nor more than ten.

ARTICLE IV

Elections

A. Officers of the Commission shall be elected at the Annual Meeting of the Commission. They shall be installed at the meeting next after their election. They shall assume their respective responsibilities and duties with the beginning of the Commission year next after their election, and these responsibilities and duties shall continue until the end of a Commission year, or until their successors assume office.

B. Elected members of the Executive Committee shall be elected by the Commission at the same meeting at which the officers are elected.

C. A nominating committee shall be appointed prior to the annual meeting, and shall nominate a slate of officers and members of the Executive Committee. Nominations from the floor shall be allowed and in order.

D. Officers and other members including one youth of the Executive Committee shall be elected for a two-year term, except in the first (1971) election. They shall serve alternate terms. In the 1971 election the terms of election of the officers and members of the Executive Committee shall be as follows:

For Two Year Terms

1. The Chairman
2. The Recording Secretary
3. The Treasurer
4. An Elected Member
5. An Elected Member

For One Year Term

1. The Vice-Chairman
2. Financial Secretary
3. An Elected Youth Member
4. An Elected Member

ARTICLE V

Project Applications

A. Applications for Commission support and or funding of any plan, project or function shall be submitted in writing to such person as authorized to receive them, and shall contain supporting information such as would enable a thorough evaluation of the application.

B. Upon receipt of all applications, the Recording Secretary shall codify, date, give serial numbers and record them in the Record Book of Applications provided for this purpose by the Commission. Applications shall then be passed on to the Committee on Plans, Projects and Priorities for investigation, evaluation and recommendation to the Executive Committee, which may make determinations and awards upon unanimous agreement in an official meeting of the Committee, or make recommendations to the Commission upon majority vote; provided, however, that any action taken or not taken in consideration of any application by the Committee shall be reported at the next meeting of the Commission.

C. All applications must be handled with as much dispatch as can reasonably be garnered. No procedure or process should be intentionally used or found to have impeded the flow of any application in the process toward final action.

ARTICLE VI

Appeals

A. A Committee on Appeals shall be created. It shall be composed of twelve members including one member elected by each of the four standing committees (excluding the By-Laws Committee), seven members elected by the Commission, and the Vice-Chairman of the Commission who shall serve as chairman of this Committee.

B. This Committee shall receive requests for appeals from actions and decisions of the Commission and its sub-bodies and shall grant hearing as it finds them proper. Its hearings shall be conducted according to design approved by the Commission. The Committee will make reports and recommendations to the Commission which shall sustain or reject them by majority vote. This report and action shall occur at the meeting of the Commission next after any hearings or denial of hearing.

ARTICLE VII

Amendments

These By-Laws may be amended by a majority vote at any regular meeting of the Commission, or special meeting called for the announced purpose of considering amendments, in the following manner:

1. The amendment shall be proposed in writing at a regular meeting and read for the information of the Commission.
2. The proposed amendment shall be duplicated and mailed to all members of the Commission at least five days before the meeting in which it is to be voted upon, and
3. The date and time of the meeting in which the amendment is to be considered is included with the amendment when mailed to the members.

Chapter XVI

Seated: Mrs. Flossie Reddick, Executive Director, Rafter's Charities and Mrs. Marjorie Brown, Executive Director, Tioga Community Youth Council. Top Row: William Brown, Coordinator, Black Panther Party and Edward McNichols, Treasurer, Open, Inc., after receiving grants.

Seated: Mrs. Gladys Bond, Director, The Center—A Place to Learn; and Mrs. Ethel Smiley, Executive Director, Bunting Friendship Freedom House, Inc. Standing: Richard W. Thompson, Director, Philadelphia Communications Center; and James Young, Director, Neighborhood Action Bureau after receiving grants.

. . . "help to people" that made a difference in their lives and in the community.

The basic structure of the Restitution Fund Commission was its "help to people" that made a difference in their lives and in the community. Like the "ripples in the ocean," it is impossible to totally gauge the influence and potential of the help provided. Suffice it to say, the money given in response to demonstrated need, and more importantly, the spirit behind the finances enhanced Philadelphia's vaunted and historic "Brotherly Love" reputation. It is a measure of extreme significance that the Church responded positively and affirmatively to these demands for assistance by "individuals of lesser means," despite the opposition of many Episcopalians that such use was outside the province of the Church, and certainly, fraught with danger and surrounded with unnecessary example setting. The reference of many, of course, was that the Church ought to be careful of its acts during precarious days of human living and, most assuredly, should follow other prominent agencies and leaders of the establishment, rather than to make a frontal attack for the solution of problems. These dissident voices who would "hang on to status quo" within the Church did not prevail. The voices that would heed the plea for succor to needy groups, projects, and individuals were followed. In so doing, the Episcopal Church, and particularly the Diocese of Pennsylvania, continued the tradition for which the Church was founded. This was the offering of a hand to those lowest on the Totem Pole in order that the whole community of God may prosper in His image and human beings may be encouraged more and more to work and perform to the upper limits of their abilities and resources.

We present here excerpts from responses to financial aid from the Restitution Fund Commission and attached to them comments explaining the uses of these funds when they were granted. All of this constitutes the historical document of which the Diocese of Pennsylvania Episcopal Church can be proud. This action will be etched forever in the history of the Church and the response of the Church.

We begin....

During the school year 1970-71, the process of decreasing and/or withdrawing of federal aid in the form of student loans, grants, and work aid in institutions of education, which was fostered by the Nixon Administration, became obvious to members of the community who were in touch with especially minority students who, because of their socio-economic status, had depended upon such aid.

In the Spring of 1971, the chairman and vice-chairman introduced to the Commission the idea of the establishment of some method through which the Commission could help meet the needs of students, especially in higher education, who were threatened with the interruption of their education because of the diminution of available assistance through the colleges.

Perhaps the brightest star in the crown of the RFC of the Diocese of Pennsylvania (indeed, if there be a crown) appears in the work done through the Education Committee, which was authorized at the Executive Committee meeting on August 31, 1971, and confirmed in the September, 1971 meeting of the Commission. The Reverend Kennth O. Grannum was appointed chairman of the Education Committee, and has served continually as its chairman. Arthur Slater, secretary-treasurer of the Committee, is credited with diligence and effectiveness in carrying out the work of the Committee, along with Mrs. Dolores Dow, Father Thomas Logan and Charles Polk (later appointed to the Committee).

Using Vice-Chairman Ridley as a consultant on procedures and the production of an application form, the Committee early decided that the most effective method of aiding students would be through contacts with financial aid offices of educational institutions, and the identification of students whose pursuit of education was "threatened by financial crisis." The Committee decided that the making of small grants rather than large continuing scholarship aid to individual students would be most effective. An application form in four copies was produced, providing a place for signed certification of the student's need by financial aid officers or by other college officials. Letters indicating the availability of student aid for threatened students were sent to college presidents, deans, and financial aid officers, especially in the Diocese of Pennsylvania and in some other colleges throughout Pennsylvania as well as along the middle Atlantic east coast.

Applications were never wanting. During the four-year period, until the end of 1975, approximately 4,000 applications were received and processed by the Committee. Six hundred grants were made to meet the educational needs of students during this four-year period. Although a very small number of grants were made up to $1,200 in very exceptional cases, the average grant was less than $300.

Grants were made to students attending eighty-five institutions. Of these institutions, 77 are post-secondary educational institutions, ranging from business and technical schools to community and junior colleges, and from four-year private and public colleges to universities and medical schools.

Of course, as would be expected, the largest number of institutions attended by those receiving grants was in Pennsylvania, this number being fourty-four. Of these grants made, approximately 500 or 83% were received by students attending these Pennsylvania institutions. Also, it is noted that 450 or 75% of the total grants were made to students attending the 26 colleges within the Diocese of Pennsylvania.

It may be of interest also to note that 450 or 75% of the grants were awarded to students attending the institutions ranking in the "top ten" in number of students receiving grants. These ten institutions in descending order include:

1. Berean Institute
2. Cheyney State College
3. Philadelphia Community College
4. Temple University
5. West Chester State College
6. Lincoln University
7. Pennsylvania State University
8. Hampton Institute
9. St. Augustine's College (North Carolina)
10. University of Pittsburgh

There were sixty-nine post-secondary students receiving grants who attended 38 institutions outside the State of Pennsylvania. These institutions are located in 18 states and the District of Columbia. They are located as far away as California, Alabama, Georgia, Louisiana, Massachusetts, Vermont, Michigan and Oklahoma.

A few grants were made to students on the secondary level. These were special grants which the Committee made for special purposes. For example, one was given to a youth who had been selected to attend a national convention of the Y.M.C.A. in San Diego, California, whose family could not finance his personal needs for such a trip. Another youth, suffering from a severe allergy, needed aid in order to take advantage of a rehabilitation program in the Bronco Junction Allergy Rehabilitation Foundation in West Virginia, and two youths were given similar grants to support their participation in the summer workshop program of the Langhorne Y.W.C.A. Additionally, there were five grants to students whose financial status threatened the possibility of their attendance at Lincoln Preparatory School, the Parkway Program, St. Joseph's Preparatory School, West Nottingham School (Maryland), and Westtown School.

Only two grants were made to students pursuing medical careers at Hahnemamn Medical College and at the Philadelphia College of Podiatry.

The list of institutions (or agencies) attended by students receiving grants, including the number of grants at each institution (appearing in parentheses), is as follows:

1. Akron, University of (1)
2. Albright College (1)
3. American University (1)
4. Antioch College, Philadelphia (1)
5. Antioch College, Vermont (Graduate School) (1)
6. Atlantic School of Hartford, Connecticut (1)
7. Berean Institute (124)
8. Boston Conservatory of Music (9)
9. Boston University (4)
10. Bristol Y.W.C.A. (1)
11. Bronco Junction Allergy Rehabilitation Foundation, West Virginia (1)
12. Bryn Mawr College (1)
13. Cabrini College (1)
14. Carnegie-Mellon Institute of Technology (1)
15. Cheyney State College (101)
16. Clarion State College (2)
17. Clark College (2)
18. Columbia University (1)
19. Combs College of Music (1)
20. Cornell University (2)
21. Dayton, University of (1)
22. Delaware State College (2)
23. Dillard University, Louisiana (1)
24. Duquesne University (1)
25. Drexell University (1)
26. Dowling College, Long Island, N.Y. (1)
27. Eastern Baptist College, St. David's (2)
28. East Stroudsburg State College (1)
29. Emerson College, Massachusetts (1)
30. Fisk University, Tennessee (2)

31. Gettysburg College (2)
32. H-N Educational Center, Philadelphia (1)
33. Hampton Institute, Virginia (6)
34. Hahnemamn Medical College (1)
35. Hartford School of Accounting, Connecticut (1)
36. Howard University, D.C. (1)
37. Immaculata College (1)
38. Indiana University of Pa. (1)
39. Lancaster, Oklahoma (1)
40. Lincoln Preparatory School, Philadelphia (1)
41. Lincoln University (9)
42. Maryland University of Eastern Shore (1)
43. Messiah College, Grantham, Pa. (1)
44. Michigan State University (3)
45. Millersville State College (3)
46. Moore College of Arts (1)
47. Montgomery County Community College (1)
48. Morehouse College, Georgia (1)
49. Morgan State College, Maryland (2)
50. Morris Brown College, Georgia (1)
51. North Carolina, A & T State University (4)
52. North Carolina Central University (1)
53. Northeastern Business School, Massachusetts (1)
54. Northeastern University, Massachusetts (1)
55. Panhandle State College, Oklahoma (1)
56. Parkway Programs, Philadelphia (1)
57. Pasadena City College, California (1)
58. Pa. College for Dietry (1)
59. Pa. State University (9)
60. Penna., University of (3)
61. Philadelphia College of Arts (4)
62. Philadelphia College of Textiles & Sciences (2)
63. Philadelphia Community College (75)
64. Philadelphia Office Training School (1)
65. Peirce Junior College (3)
66. Pittsburgh, University of (5)
67. Rutgers, the State University, N.J. (1)
68. Rochester Institute of Technology (2)
69. St. Joseph's Preparatory School (1)
70. St. Joseph's College (1)
71. St. Augustine's College, N.C. (6)
72. Skidmore College, N.Y. (1)
73. South Carolina, University of (1)
74. Spring Garden Institute, Philadelphia (1)
75. Syracuse University, N.Y. (4)
76. Temple University (65)
77. Tuskegee Institute, Alabama (1)
78. Upsala College, N.J. (1)
79. Visual Arts Institute, N.Y. (1)

80. West Chester State College (48)
81. West Nottingham Academy, Maryland (1)
82. Westtown School (1)
83. Widner College (2)
84. X-Ray Technology School, Philadelphia General Hospital (1)
85. Y.W.C.A. Workshop Summer Programs (2)

The extent of the work of the Educational Committee is obvious from a reading of the data above. On the other hand, attention should be called to the fact that each entry in this compilation represents much time and effort on the part of the volunteers who were members of the Commission and who gave their time and energies to the receipt, reading, evaluations and decision-making process with regard to making awards to these students and at these many institutions. The widespread public relations effect of such an activity is clearly seen by the insightful reader. On the other hand, there is another side to the picture and this is the more important. What are the responses of the officers of the institutions, of parents, of students, of friends and others to this effort to minimize the threat of financial crisis in the lives of these young people? A conservative estimate indicates that 1,300 letters and responses were received in connection with the 600 or more awards which were made. In some instances, several letters were received regarding one award: from officers of institutions, from parents and from ministers or from the students themselves.

Let us now look at some of the responses which have been received in order that the reader might evaluate for himself and share some of the feelings of the various respondents to this effort:

April 6, 1972

"...Your kind grant will certainly be of material advantage to each of these young men in their scholastic endeavors."

WILLIAM M. PATTERSON
Counselor, Lincoln University

June 20, 1972

"...On behalf of the President, Dr. Roy D. Hudson, and the members of the Financial Aid Committee, I want to thank you and the members of the Commission for your interest and support of Miss Hill."

RHOMIE L. HECK, JR.
Director, Finannial Affairs, Hampton Institute

January 30, 1973

"...We sincerely appreciate your interest in this young man and we feel that he, too, is grateful for your generous contribution toward his educational expense. Best wishes."

J. MILLS HOLLOWAY
Vice President for Financial Affairs, St. Augustine's College

January 30, 1973

"Thank you very much for the $300 check for Robert Downey. He is a fine young man and is doing well here at the Academy. I think your investment has been well made. Thank you again."

KENNETH E. DIETRICH
Headmaster, West Nottingham Academy

February 26, 1973

"... to express my thanks for the check which you recently sent to Clarion State College to be used for educational expenses of Betsy Herndon. Since we have to defend our state and federal funds, we really appreciate it when grants such as yours are made available to our students."

ROBERT C. SEGEBARTH
Director, Financial Aid, Clarion State College

February 27, 1973

"... This check has been placed on deposit with the college bank against the $375 tuition fee which is due from James Jones. James has assured us that as soon as he can raise the money, he will pay the other amount which is due."

I. G. LEWIS
Administrative Dean, Pasadena City College

March 13, 1973

"... I am familiar with Mr. Fuller's financial program, and I know that this $300 made a critical difference in his ability to remain at the University this semester. I, therefore, add my appreciation to his for this most helpful gift and would appreciate your sharing our expression with members of the Educational Committee."

(Mrs.) E. L. EDWARDS
Director, Financial Aid, Fisk University

June 11, 1973

"... This check will be deposited in our scholarship fund and made available to Sabrina K. Herrington in accordance with your recommendation. We wish to commend your organization on this aid to one of our students."

WILLIAM M. SRSIC
Assistant Director of Financial Aid, Indiana University of Pa.

August 6, 1973

"... The educational grants (2) of $200 each will be a great help to the students in defraying the costs of obtaining an education. Thank you and your committee for your interest and assistance.

SISTER MARIA CHRISTA
Financial Aid Officer, Immaculata College

September 18, 1973

We are pleased that your assistance will keep Miss Davis in our department of Theatre at the University of South Carolina and trust that she will have a profitable year.

FRANCIS COUNTS
Graduate School Office, University of South Carolina

September 21, 1973

On behalf of the faculty committee on scholarships, grants, and loans, I would like to thank the RFC of the Episcopal Diocese of Pennsylvania for the scholarship contribution for two Drexell students.

JOHN R. MCCULLOUGH
Director of Student Financial Aid, Drexell University

January 3, 1974

"...We appreciate your financial support in providing Miss Russell an educational opportunity."

(Mrs.) I. B. JONES
Student Financial Aid Director, Morris Brown College

April 1, 1974

"...On behalf of the Institute and this office, may I extend to you our sincere appreciation for your interest in our students."

S. DOUGLAS HOOVER
Director of Student Aid, Rochester Institute of Technology

October 8, 1974

"...May I take this opportunity to express our congratulations to you for recognizing the vital need for student scholarship support, especially in an era when educational costs continue to spiral."

GARY A. LEE
Director, Cornell University

The trustees of the University of Pennsylvania gratefully acknowledge receipt of $300 from the RFC of the Episcopal Diocese of Pennsylvania. This remittance has been credited to the account of Rita Hudson—academic year 1974-75.

ROBERT D'AUGUSTINE
Sponsor Scholarship Officer, University of Pennsylvania

"...You and your Commission have the deep gratitude of all of us here at the college who are concerned with the education of women. Such assistance as you provide is surely needed and much appreciated. I feel certain that Miss Hicks will live up to the trust you place in her.

SISTER ELIZABETH MCNAMARA
Financial Aid Officer, Rosemont College

April 17, 1975

"...It is becoming a genuine problem for us to meet the ever increasing financial needs of our students. Therefore, on behalf of the University, may I take this opportunity to express our deepest appreciation for your scholarship.

SUSAN S. DIPTERLINE
Assistant Director and Coordinator, Scholarship/Grant Division, Syracuse University

March 25, 1975

On behalf of West Chester State College and our students, I thank you and the Commission for your financial support. . . ." "A copy of our current undergraduate catalog is being sent to you under separate cover for your information and reference."

THEODORE H. BUTCHER
Director, Financial Aid, West Chester State College

STUDENTS EXPRESS THEMSELVES

October 27, 1972

". . . I cannot express my gratitude for the money you have given me. It is greatly appreciated, and will help to defray some of my college expenses. I thank you very much again.

GAYLE M. WATKINS

September 22, 1972

I would like to thank you for awarding me $300 for the first half of my semester. I am so much in need of help. I have another grant of $400 for the second semester. I got a job in the school too and it pays about $300, but all of this is not enough, so I would like and appreciate it if you could help me in any way toward the second semester. Thank you very much.

QUINCY MARSHALL, JR.

October 3, 1972

". . . I want to express my feeling of appreciation to the fund for the grant that was made to me. I can now continue my education at West Chester State College. . . " "Thanks again!"

CAROL WILSON

October 10, 1973

The notification that my funds had arrived at Community College was very, very welcome. I am sure that when the school opens, those funds will make my educational burdens much lighter. I would like to thank all those who had a hand in assisting me.

KENNETH BARNES

November 1, 1972

". . . I want to thank you and your committee for your efforts in obtaining fees for my higher education. . . " "Your concern for my education is and will always be appreciated. Once again, I say THANK YOU!"

PRESTON BELLINGER, JR.

January 31, 1972

I would sincerely like to thank you for helping me to continue my college career for the year 1972-73. I will endeavor, to the best of my ability, to keep a high academic average here at St. Augustine's College and, again, I would like to thank you and the RFC for helping me this year. Thank you again.

DONALD L. MOORE

October 23, 1972

I would like to thank the RFC for your most appreciated help. You all have made it possible for me to complete what I hope will be a rewarding course here at Berea. I cannot seem to find the correct words to thank you for what you have done..." "This is just to say that I appreciate your help, for in as much as you have helped me, I have endeavored to help myself."

BARBARA WELEN

October 3, 1972

My name is Dorothy Lowe. I am a student attending the Hartford Institute of Accounting, located in Hartford, Connecticut. My grades are very good and this school of accounting is an excellent school. I will be graduating in May of 1973..." "My purpose in writing this letter is to give you a brief note of appreciation for the $300 lump sum that was sent to HIA for my financial aid. You have helped me more than you realize..."

DOROTHY LOWE

February 9, 1973

"...I would like for you to know that the money was dearly needed and wisely used..." "I am now in my last semester of Industrial Photography curriculum at the Philadelphia Community College and I expect to graduate in June of this year. Your small grant helped me immensely.

STEVE PRESLEY

February 28, 1973

I am writing this letter thanking you for your youth and your RFC of the Episcopal Diocese of Pennsylvania for the money you have contributed to my education at St. Joseph's College. I do very much appreciate it, and will make every effort to utilize every penny to pursue my major field of interest..." "Once again, thank you very much for your consideration in my case."

LONGO KOLOKIHAKAUFISI

March 9, 1973

I would like to thank the RFC for the scholarship which helped my educational courses this semester here at Clarion State College..." "Without the money, I could not have completed the semester..."

BETSY HERNDON

April 25, 1973

I wish to thank you and the Educational Committee of the RFC for the grant given to me so that I can continue my education. It will help me indeed. With the funds I will be able to attend summer school.

MS. LAVERNE COLEMAN

April 25, 1973

"Thank you very much for the money that was given toward my education. This money will be a great help to me in completing this year at Penn State University. . . "

MICHAEL

April 27, 1973

I have received the $400 awarded me by the Educational Committee. My heart-filled gratitude goes out to everyone for the help you have given to fund my education. This assistance was most beneficial.

MRS. CLARICE FORD

May 7, 1973

"I sincerely want to thank you from the bottom of my heart. The financial assistance through the Education Committee that I have received, I shall never forget. . . I should have taken time long before now though, but, with term papers and final exams behind me now this is the first chance I've had. . . Thank you very much again."

MAUDE T. HARRIS

May 12, 1973

"This letter is written with deep appreciation and my most sincere gratitude for the assistance made available to me by your organization. . . I would like to thank you and the Educational Committee for your concern and rapid action, concerning my request for financial assistance. It is very comforting to know that there are wonderful, caring human beings such as yourselves, who are interested in helping students; regardless of race, religion or creed. Thank you ever so much."

LEE J. SAUNDERS

May 13, 1973

". . . My sincerest thanks for the generous award. . ." "You have made it possible for me to continue my studies this school year with a lot more financial stability. Thank you."

VALERIE J. HARRIS

July 16, 1973

"This is something I should have done earlier. I'm sorry, but my feelings are still the same. I can't seem to find words to express myself so I hope a THANK YOU KINDLY can help. Also your material help was a prayer answered."

MARK THOMPSON

June 23, 1973

"Thank you very much for contributing toward my education

at Cheyney State College. The money was needed and is most appreciated. I thank you again."

THERESA F. CRIPEN

June 24, 1973

"Many thanks for the money that arrived just in time for me to attend summer school..." "God bless and thank you very much."

FRANCES L. ROBINSON

July 23, 1973

"...I am sending this note to you as a small part of my very deep gratitude. This money will now enable me to purchase my textbooks and materials for school in the fall. Once again, my deep thanks to you!"

THERESA FUISON

July 25, 1973

"...Words cannot express my appreciation for being one of the recipients. I will work diligently to do my best during the school year.... Thank you again for being so considerate in helping me meet the financial requirements needed in attending Cheyney State College."

MRS. VIOLA REDD

August 7, 1973

"I am writing to thank you and all concerned in the decision for a grant which you have kindly donated in my favor towards my fees at Cheyney State College. This is not just a little relief to me! I shall ever remain grateful and thankful for any assistance that is given me. Thank you ever so much for your kindness."

O. J. ESTE

October 10, 1973

"I would like to thank you for the $200 grant awarded to me, to help while pursuing my education here at North Carolina Central University. I am most appreciative and sure it will be of great assistance to me. Thank you again very much."

JOCELYN F. PERRY

October 19, 1973

"...I am most deeply grateful to you and your committee who agreed to help me. I am now back in school and doing well.... You may be sure that I am working hard to prove worthy of your kind trust in me... and thank you again and again."

JA'ALA MCNEIL

March 29, 1974

"...This has been a great relief to me.... Thank you very much and may God bless you all."

OFFIONG JETTE

"...I will be completing this semester and re-enrolling in the fall semester as a full time student at Moore College of Art. I can assure you that your investment has been a sound one, and again I thank you and your committee for your assistance."

ELYSE V. BRADT

April 7, 1974

"...This is only to thank you and to tell you that it means a lot to me not to have to struggle to pay my tuition for the next two months. Again thanks to you and the Commission."

BERNICE S. BROTHERS

April 23, 1974

"...I wish to thank you and all the other people who have made the Commission possible and hope that you can continue to assist others as you have so generously assisted me."

JUDITH C. JONES

June 18, 1974

"...I'm truly grateful because it is a privilege for a person to acquire a higher education and your concern has been duly appreciated.... I pray that someday I will attain my goal and prove worthy of it. Thank you again."

GLADYS V. LOCKMAN

November 12, 1974

"...The money I received was very helpful...." "I pray for God's blessings on your efforts. May you continue to bring hope and understanding to students like me. Thank you again."

GEORGIE STUBBS

November 19, 1974

"I am very much indebted to you and your Committee for seeing me as a worthy beneficiary from your fund.... My entire family and I extend our unlimited gratitude to you and the founders of the Restitution Fund. You have rallied round to rescue me from drowning. May the organization grow from strength to strength. May all by whose financial contributions I have benefited and you whose decision has calmed my anxiety, be rewarded by

Christ who is the author of goodness and mercy.... Accept my immense thanks."

JOSEPH O. E. OHANUGO
Lincoln University

January 23, 1975

"...I am now completing my sophomore year at Community College and will be enrolled at Temple University beginning as a junior in the fall of this year. I must admit that it has not been easy, considering my responsibilities. However, I am determined to reach my goal in a matter of a couple of years. Through my determination, I have been fortunate to achieve honor roll status and with my continued health and God's help I hope to persist in this manner.... Thank you once again for your consideration in my endeavors."

GLORIA A. PITTS

January 30, 1975

"...It came in a very good time just when I needed money for my books and materials for this semester. I very much appreciate it and I can assure you that every last penny of it will be put to very good use...." "During hard times like this, it is very comforting to know that there are still some people who are still willing to give out something to help others. I wish you and the Commission the best of everything. May your efforts be rewarded. Once again I say thank you and God Bless you."

MERLE ASHIE

June 19, 1972

"We received a copy of the grant for my son at East Stradsburg State College...." "I am writing to thank you and the Restitution Fund Commission for your willingness to help us. It is well appreciated and we needed it very much. God bless and keep you. Thanks again and again."

SELMA H. MANIGO
(Mother of Stephen H. Manigo)

October 10, 1972

"I am Mrs. Helen M. Wright, age 31, mother of two children. Yes, I have been away from Overbrook High School for quite a number of years. I am a June 1959 graduate." "...At this time, I would like to thank you for giving me the opportunity to return to school and once again to pursue my education. I am enjoying my classes here at Berean and look forward to every evening. This has been indeed an opportunity for me. Once again, I thank you."

HELEN M. WRIGHT

October 4, 1972

"Our family would like to take this opportunity to thank the Commission for an award to Jeffrey, to help finance his college education at Hampton Institute for 1972-73."

MRS. HENRY R. JACKSON, SR.

October 15, 1972

"Thank you very much for your generous gift from the Restitution Fund Commission. . . . " "This will help my tuition cost for next semester and with these tuition costs out of the way it will make things easier for my wife and family. Thank you again for your consideration."

RONALD S. COLEMAN

October 23, 1973

"We are writing to offer to you and the Restitution Fund Commission our grateful appreciation for the funds which were given through the Reverend Bruce B. Williamson to help with sending us to Palmer Institute. . . . We want you to know we are in college and enjoying our studies. Again, thanking you, we are sincerelyyours.

GEORGIA BUTLER
LEOLA BUTLER
NORMA FERGUSON
ROSEMARY ARMBISTER

January 26, 1975

". . . The above check was a pleasant and welcomed surprise as a mid-term tuition for my other children also falls due now. This check could not have been sent at a better time as I was wondering how I was going to pay Susan's balance at school. Thank you again. Most sincerely,

HELEN L. HICKS
(Mother)

February 7, 1975

"I would sincerely like to thank you and your organization for approving my request for funding. I am a widow, with two small children, trying to meet mortgage payments and other obligations —I can't begin to tell you how desperately I needed $150 to purchase books and supplies to help me with my schooling. Again, thank you and God bless you."

SHIRLEY HAMILTON

"I am writing this letter to thank you for the award to further my education at the Community College in Philadelphia. I appreciate it very much and would be grateful if you could send me an application for next semester. I asked my Priest Reverend John

Studabaker and Mrs. Parker of the St. Barnabas Church to give their personal thanks for the award you have given me."

ALFREDIA PARKER

The major work of the RFC consisted of the receipt and the evaluation of applications from community institutions and agencies and the making of decisions with regard to which of these projects would be funded and to what extent. Applications from community agencies were abundantly present, almost overwhelmingly so. Funds requested and applications received by the Commission during the first year amounted to $1.4 million. In the first five years of its existence the Commission is estimated to have received applications amounting to $6 million from community agencies.

The effectiveness of the RFC in carrying out its function must be evaluated on the basis of the types of agencies funded and the purposes of the funding. For convenience and discussion the programs and projects which received grants from the Commission have been divided into eight rough categories. These are based upon the types of projects and especially upon the purposes to be served by the grants. It is recognized that some of the projects could easily be placed in two or three categories. In fact, almost every project could be placed in more than one category.

GRANTS FOR DEVELOPMENTAL PURPOSES

Grants for developmental purposes were given generally to already existing agencies for support of some specific addition to the program or purposes of the organization or to improve the financial stability of the agency. This was the largest of the categories.

There were twenty-eight grants made for developmental purposes for a total of $134,337. A variety of agencies and institutions were assisted. The agencies used the funds granted for many purposes, including: purchase of instruments for a group of young people with musical talent in order to provide employment for them; the support of the development of places where young jazz artists could appear; and training of plumbers, electricians, household workers and truck drivers. The provision of community youth activities, the support of worthwhile new type, struggling businesses, the support of programs designed to improve learning in high school students as well as adults and the provision of centers for the coordination and stimulation of mutually beneficial community activity were additional uses for which the grant money was used. Some examples of specific programs supported in this category were the Philadelphia Communications Center which received a grant of $3,000 to help with rent and other expenses in connection with housing and Ombudsman program. This project handled over 5,000 requests for information, complaints, and help with problems; or the North Central Unity, an agency, which received a grant of $5,000 to help purchase basic materials to construct the interior of their building and to purchase some equipment to house their North Philadelphia Community in Child Care Services and services to Senior Citizens.

The Amalgamated Plumbers and Junior Electricians received grants of approximately $4,000 each to support and improve their programs in aiding young blacks in apprenticeships for these trades. The Advocate Community Development Corporation received a grant for $7,000 in support of education and stimulation in North Philadelphia areas to induce blacks to participate in and benefit from programs of purchasing of new housing and rehabilitation of housing. In one phase, ACDC reported success in forty-six instances. The Tyoga Community Youth Council received two grants equaling $7,000 for development of programs of tutoring and community activities.

Father Bruce Williamson was granted $5,000 to secure scholarships and grants for Bahamian students to attend several colleges in the United States. The Commission supported a Communications Workshop at Temple University for introduction and orientation of young black people to opportunities in the communications field. The Center—A Place To Learn, and the Philadelphia Adult Basic Education Project received grants for the provision of tutoring programs in their respective communities. The Neighborhood Action Bureau received a grant for $4,000 with which it was able to purchase materials for the renovation of a building which now serves as its center for its neighborhood improvement program and its youth recreation program. These and other projects received small grants which gave impetus and stability to projects which were in difficulty. Recent conversations and visits indicate that most of these agencies were still functioning in their communities and their programs have solidified.

SERVICES TO CHILDREN

In the category of services to children are included fourteen grants in the amount of $73,400. Among the agencies which received grants were several day care centers including East Frankfort Day Care Center, Kensington Self Help Center and Marie Lea Child Care Center. These three agencies received a total of $19,500 to aid in matching funds which were required in order to receive State and/or Federal funds as well as to purchase materials and services. The Bunting Friendship Freedom House received grants totaling $4,500 for its Child Care programs.

Other programs supported included Rafters Charity which received $7,500 for its general services to children. BEDC (Black Economic Development Conference) received two grants totaling $8,500 to support summer programs of education and recreation for children and the Pennsylvania Chapter of the Black Panther Party Breakfast Program was helped in the amount of $3,000. Two other programs in this category were the Women's Christian Alliance which received $5,000 in support of foster home program and Children's Services which received $20,000 in budgetary crisis in support of a program of adoption.

The Pennsylvania Eastern District Camping Foundation which improved its grounds and provided summer camping for children from Center City received $5,000.

CHURCHES AND RELIGIOUS ORGANIZATIONS

The next largest number of grants consists of the nine grants made to religious institutions. All grants made to churches are included in this category as well as the one $5,000 grant made to the Institute of Black Ministries for support of its library improvement program. The average grant in this category was approximately $8,000. The three largest grants of $15,000 each were awarded to St. Philip's Memorial Church for renovations required for a day care center, to St. Augustine's Church of the Covenant in support of the development of a youth program, and to Calvary Northern Liberties Church for renovation and equipment for a community playground. Grants of lesser amounts were given to St. Barnabas Episcopal School ($6,000) and to St. Simon the Cyrenian ($8,000). Grants of less than $3,000 were given to the Church of our Savior and The Church of Holy Apostles and Mediator for renovation to improve facilities for community use, and to All Souls Mission for the Deaf for the purchase of auditory equipment.

GRANTS TO ORGANIZED EDUCATIONAL AGENCIES

Five grants fall in this category and they average $6,200. These included a $6,000 grant to Wilberforce University, a Methodist institution in Ohio, which suffered a severe emergency following destruction left by a tornado. Two grants totaling $15,000 were made to the Alice Rouse Donaldson Educational Self Help Center in South Philadelphia for the purchase of equipment and materials for its program which is operated in cooperation with the Philadelphia Public Schools and for the provision of teacher aides to assist in its programs. The Opportunities Industrialization Center was granted $7,000 for purchase of air conditioning equipment which was required to convert a poorly ventilated facility into classroom facilities so that classes could be held during the summer.

GANG AND DRUG CONTROL

Pennsylvania Program for Women and Girl Offenders was given a grant of $6,000 for printing, materials and program. Neighborhood Crusades, Inc. received a grant of $2,500 for the purchase of a vehicle to carry its program to the community. The West Park Community Action Center received a grant of $6,000 for its program and the House of Umoja received a grant of $5,000 for the purchase of property for its program.

HEALTH SERVICES

Four grants were made in this category averaging approximately $3,900. The Grace Ferry Multipurpose Center received two grants totaling $10,000 for the purchase of equipment. The Sickle Cell Anemia Research Agency received a grant of $2,500 and The Young Great Society of Medical Services received a grant of $3,000 for its programs.

RECREATIONAL

A grant of $1,500 was given to Black Butterfly, an organization of young people who needed instruments for their program of presentation of Street, Music and Drama. The Youth Community Project of St. Andrews and St. Monica Church received a grant of $5,000. The West Chester Community Center received a grant of $3,000 for erection of a new facility and the St. John's Settlement House received $2,500.

VOTER REGISTRATION AND EDUCATION

Three grants were awarded in this category. The Committee of One Thousand and the NAACP received grants of $1,000 each to stimulate voter registration. The Voter Education Project of North Philadelphia received a grant of $5,000 for the encouragement of voter registration and for continuing a Voter Education Project.

The previous descriptions give some feeling and information for the projects which were supported and some data base for construction of objective and precise appraisal of the work of the Restitution Fund Commission.

The responses of the persons who were responsible for the work of the agencies and institutions to which grants were made constitute a valid appraisal of the real effectiveness of the work of the Restitution Fund Commission. The Commission and its work were imbedded deeply in the Christian spirit. The responses of people supersede the data of the amounts of money given and types of projects supported.

RESPONSES TO THE GRANTS MADE BY THE RESTITUTION FUND COMMISSION

Beginning in the spring of 1975 the Committee on Historical Records of the Restitution Fund Commission designed a questionnaire for collecting objective information on the results of the work of the Commission. The materials included three covering letters and a questionnaire which contained five items of inquiry. The covering letters were addressed to three populations. The five items of inquiry contained in the questionnaire were as follows:

I. What general values (such as moral, encouragement, etc.) came to your work or program because of the financial aid received by the Restitution Fund Commission?

II. What failures occurred because of the receipt of funds or despite this? Was there something the Commission could have done to ward off the failure?

III. What specific benefits were made possible through the funds from the Commission which would not have been possible without these funds?

IV. Describe any one or more cases in which persons were helped directly in their lives because of the funds received from the Commission.

V. What overall evaluation (praise and/or criticism) based on the activities of the Diocese of Pennsylvania or the Restitution Fund Commission do you have?

A prepaid envelope was enclosed for return.

The distribution of the questionnaires included three groups: all members and former members of the Restitution Fund Commission (42), agencies and institutions which had received grants from the Restitution Fund Commission (71), and selected key participants in the work of the Diocese (278), the latter group included 155 clergymen and 123 laypersons. All of the clergymen were selected from the key mailing list of the Diocesan office, and the lay persons were selected mostly from this list, with a few additions. The laypersons included officers, council members and committeemen of the Diocese, senior wardens of the Parishes, and some other individuals known to be acquainted with the work of the Commission.

A total of 135 or 34% of the 391 questionnaires were returned. The returns from the respective groups show 23 or 55% returns from members or former members of the Commission, 39 or 55% from agencies and institutions which received grants, and 73 or 22% returned from the selected participants in the work of the Diocese of Pennsylvania.

It is generally accepted knowledge that in dealing with questionnaires a return of 55% is considered as high or very good. A return of 22% is considered as acceptable.

While on the subject of information gathering the authors believe it well to interpose here that in addition to information gathered through the use of questionnaires other information has been gathered. Tapes and notes record interviews with 46 persons. These interviews extended in length up to two hours. Interviews of at least an hour were held with Bishop Dewitt, Father Blackburn, Father Washington, Father Hawkins and with Messrs. Pilgrim, Harburger, and Kenyatta. Included are some contacts which were expedited in seven to ten minute telephone conversations. Among other persons interviewed are counted priests and lay members of the commission, some of whom stayed and some of whom departed, and officers of some agencies and institutions which received grants.

Let us now return to the major thrust of this chapter. What were the responses of individuals who returned questionnaires? How did they feel about the RFC and the results of its work?

Responses from Agencies and Institutions

By design and purpose the RFC was established with the goal of development and sponsoring, within and for the black community, of such programs and projects as arise from their self-determined aims and purposes, and as will result in benefit to the community in the areas of its economic, political, educational and social well-being. Perhaps there would be agreement upon the assumption that the most vigorous, significant and valid test of the work of the commission is obtained in the responses and evaluations of the leaders of the institution and agencies to which aid was given.

The questionnaire's first inquiry was "What general values came to your work or program because of the financial aid received from the Restitution Fund Commission?"

It is literally impossible to describe the responses of the representatives from the agencies and institutions to this question. Half the associations and concepts are lost in transcription to the printed page. Indeed, every respondent indicated clearly that considerable and in most cases multiple values accrued to the programs because of the aid received from the commission. According to the statements some programs were saved, others were made capable of continuing on a self-help basis, and in many morale heightened greatly. There was increased interest on the part of boards, participants or workers, and there was heightened belief that groups could make positive change. Some groups felt an affirmation of their own efforts as worthwhile, some were able to initiate new programs which they had hoped for, some were able to rectify conditions which were threats to safety, some were able to expand the outreach of their programs, some were able to provide services for parents which allowed the parents to work, and some volunteer groups which were about to "fold" took on revitalized interest and carried programs forward. Some reported the boosting of morale in the black community thru the establishment of a project designed to satisfy their needs. Increased learning and participation on the part of students and parents is reported. Ecumenical values were reported in two instances.

Although it is impossible to include all of the responses to the first inquiry or to include all of what most of the respondents have written regarding this question, some quotations are submitted:

> "The grant received from the RFC was used as matching funds to keep the Day Care Service program operating. (The program is designed to assist school age parents in continuing their education and entering into the world of work.)
>
> ...The program served 92 families with infants and toddlers between the ages of 2 weeks and three years. Raising the 25% matching funds annually presented a major frustrating, threatening prob-

lem. . . it is impossible to describe the reaction to the grant. It was received at a time when we were at the Wits End Corner (SEC) trying to generate matching funds. You responded to our appeal at a time when it was most necessary. We are sincerely thankful."

MRS. EVELYN A. FRAZIER
Tyoga Community Youth Council

". . . The grant received from the RFC enabled the Neighborhood Action Bureau to purchase and to partly renovate its building at 2644 N. Hutchinson Street, and did indeed help the Neighborhood Action Bureau to continue its program from a self help platform."

JAMES F. YOUNG
Director, Neighborhood Action Bureau

"The grant was received at a very critical time when there was a shortage of funds for the Social Service Program at Open. Through this support the program continued uninterrupted and continues today."

EDWARD MCNICHOL
Open, Incorporated

"The Board has taken an increased interest in the welfare and needs of the community and become more involved with Kings Village. . . . The funds enabled Holy Communion to obtain a get set day care center—the only facility of its kind in this immediate area. . . the ethnic heritage affairs institute organized a neighborhood center which operates from the old clinic facility in the basement of the hall . . . both have been a great help in meeting the needs of the community. . . the food buying club operated by the neighborhood center has been a real help to many of our elderly and poor by enabling them to purchase good fresh food (especially produce and, lately, meats) at a good savings over store prices."

BARTON D. BERRY, JR.
Greys Ferry Multi Purpose Center

"A tremendous boost in morale was effected by the grant from the Episcopal Diocese RFC to our organization. The funds were sorely needed to complete and furnish our initial building at Gibraltor, Pennsylvania. . . . The grant was historical in that it marked the first time a contribution of this size was tendered from one major denomination to the work and efforts initiated by another."

W. HOWARD JONES
Pennsylvania Eastern District; Congress Camping Foundation, Inc.

"The Youth Committee, which was at a low ebb, were most encouraged through receipt of the RFC grant. This enabled them to project a respectable working program which would keep boys and young men off the city streets and away from gang activities. The boys expressed gratitude for your consideration of their needs."

CHESTER MONTAGUE, *Director*
The Youth Recreation Program, St. Andrews and St. Monica

"We were able to produce a film on local race and the local prison system, which provided a focus for our task force and caused it to remain active and interested in the problem. . . without the funds our film would not have been made. Now we have a reasonably professional looking film of race and the prisons which is available for others to see. It provides an excellent introduction to the problems of incarceration, particularly as they affect blacks, and raises issues that transcend the immediate circumstances shown in the film."

JOHN SHELLENBERGER
Prison Task Force

The above responses to the first question, on the general values which came to the work of these organizations and agencies as a result of financial aid received from the RFC, it seems, bear close inspection. A generous sampling of responses is provided purposely. It is suggested that the answers to this inquiry and to inquiry number five are crucial and pivotal in aiding the reader, if he decides to evaluate the work of the commission.

The second inquiry in the questionnaire asked what failures occurred because of the receipt of funds, or despite this. Was there something that the Commission could have done to ward off the failure? The responses to this query in general indicated that there were no failures so far as the projects were concerned, and so far as the Commission was concerned. On the other hand, there were from time to time statements that although there really were no failures, there was impatience caused by delays in receiving funds after applications, or that plans had to be changed because of changing circumstances or needs. In every instance it was indicated that the Commission could not have done anything to ward off the inconvenience. It should be said that there were only three or four discussions under this item. Additionally, however, it was indicated that in many instances increased grants would have been valuable or more helpful to the agencies or institutions. It might be of interest to note that three of the individuals who responded congratulated the Commission on the promptness of attention to the application and the granting of funds. Suffice it to say that fund granting agencies in general do not have the reputation for quickness and promptness.

Item three in the questionnaire raises the question of specific benefits made possible through the funds from the Commission, which would not have been possible without these funds. This is an extension of question number one. Item four in the questionnaire requested a description of any one or more individual cases in which persons were helped directly in their lives because of funds received from the commission.

These items, number three and four, will be treated together since they both give specific instances of benefits to programs or individuals. Relatively few of the many, many specific instances described in response to the questionnaire will be included as samples.

> "The following benefits, which would not have been at all possible otherwise, were made possible through the funds from the Commission. The provision of an adequate office for NAB, a recreational facility where boxing, Karate is taught to our youngsters plus an all purpose recreational and meeting center for use of all people of the surrounding community regardless of race, creed or color. Also because of these improvements our case load of community service has doubled."*
>
> JAMES F. YOUNG
> *Director, Neighborhood Action Bureau*

> "... The following activities:
>
> A. distribution of emergency food and clothing
> B. individual and family counseling
> C. work with tenants council organization
> D. participation in welfare rights organization
>
> Assistance with a family recently arrived from Puerto Rico in the following:
>
> A. placed in temporary housing adjacent to Open's office.
> B. supplied with emergency food
> C. assistance in locating permanent housing

---

*(In describing individual cases in which persons were helped directly, the Neighborhood Action Bureau's response to the questionnaire includes the names and the old address and new address for each of twenty six families who have moved into homes purchased and renovated through cooperative neighborhood action. Among the pictures at various points in this book are found two pictures called "before" and "after" showing houses before and after renovation. These are actual pictures taken on a visit to the NAB. On this visit, Mr. Young, the Director of NAB said "the RFC's grant came as we were just getting ready to close. We did not see how we could continue to exist without support. The RFC saved us!")

D. accompanied parents to DPA office to apply for public assistance—payments and foodstamps."

EDWARD J. MCNICHOL
Open, Inc.

"You said it! Seventy community groups plus five hundred students whose organizational and personal careers were "saved." God is using the RFC!"*

"That would take a book!"**

MUHAMMAD KENYATTA
BEDC, Inc., (Children's Summer Program)

"Because of the grant by the RFC, the Prisoners Rights Council was able to carry out its program for the 1972-73 year. This resulted in the first real changes in the prison system affected by PRC. This included the implementation of an indefinite moratorium on experimentation (involving prisoners) in Pennsylvania. In addition, we testified before Senator Edward Kennedy's sub-committee on health in regard to medical experimentation, thereby contributing to ending medical experimentation on a national level.

"Furthermore, we gathered supporting facts regarding declarations of prisoners rights in disciplinary hearings, executive clemency, prisoner transfers, etc.

"In addition, PRC during the 1972-73 year began to actively work on its voting rights project, which resulted in unconvicted inmates in the state of Pennsylvania being granted the right to vote in September, 1974. PRC is the only organization that actively handles requests from inmates and their families concerning the positive benefits of this service through 1972-73.

"In addition, the entire population of Philadelphia County prisons and the state prisons of Pennsylvania have been positively affected as the result of changes in the prison system which our projects have brought about (because of the grant made by the RFC)."

ALLAN H. LAWSON
Executive Director, The Prisoners Rights Council, Inc.

---

*(This is perhaps the most interesting of the comments received in the questionnaires returned. In the covering letters, we indicated that approximately seventy grants had been made and more than five hundred students had received grants. The response to item three on specific benefits was made on the basis of the covering letter.)

**(In answer to item four which asks for one or more individual cases helped directly.)

". . . We were able to establish two more classrooms. . . more play and work area for children and teachers. . . complete renovation of one building—indoor and outdoor play equipment. . . science room with live animals and plants, texts and unusual materials dealing with the child's environment, through which the child develops a love and sense of responsibility to all living creatures. . . a summer swimming and recreation program was instituted with stress on developing social and physical skills at an earlier age than normally occurs.

". . . Two families were helped. . . one mother with two children was allowed to stay on premises for eight months. The younger child was taken care of during the day and the teenage daughter was given a job after school hours. She worked as an aide in the center. . . the second family was having domestic problems. The child was allowed to receive free care for a month until the problem could be solved."

MRS. EILEEN SLAUGHTER
Maria Lea Community Child Center

". . . . and with news of the grant, pledges were re-newed by the students and the membership to donate materials and labor to complete the first floor of the school and the upper floors. . . we were able to complete the first floor rear of our building. This has given us space for an additional theory class.

There are many other examples of successful gains made by our students, but these two are perhaps of special note:

A. Mr. Lennox Hinkson, initially a very good student, took advantage of the newly added mechanical drawing classes. . . passed the city of Philadelphia Journeymans Plumbing Test . . . became gainfully employed in the plumbing trade with wages approximating union scale. . . is now a volunteer theory instructor of Almagamated's Friday night class.

B. Mr. Roger Williams—was one of the first students to attend the mechanical drawing and theory classes. Hence, it was with great pleasure that we recommended Roger for employment at the Delaware State Department of Public Instruction, where he is now employed as an instructor in the training of young men in the field of plumbing. He is now a volunteer mathematics instructor."

BRUCE F. HOUSTON
Almagamated Plumbers Association of Philadelphia

". . . All the workshop students indicated that they had learned or gained information of value regarding the communications field. . . . I am certain that at least four workshop students gained determination to learn more about mass communications, with the possible intention of working toward careers in communications fields. On the other hand, at least two of the students determined that they could serve society better in other fields."

BRUCE UNDERWOOD
Communications Workshop, Temple University

"All of the participants in our program in one way or another were greatly helped. There were at least three children between the ages of two weeks and 2 months at our center. To our knowlege, no other center took children this young. If the doors had been closed the parents would have been forced to drop out of school, therefore, in their particular cases the purpose of the entire program would have been defeated... through your grant the doors of the Day Care Services were kept ajar to allow continued services to child and parents."

MRS. ALDENE A. FRAZIER
The Tyoga Youth Council

"Follow-up on-the-job counseling to graduates would have been more limited without the grant... part of the grant helped support the publishing of a book of case histories (including twenty pages of case histories of those who were particularly helped by the grants)... it helped us on our most difficult journey—changing the value rating of the service occupation in our society."

MRS. UVELIA S. A. BOWEN
Employment Association for Re-Evaluation and Training

"As a result of your grant and the purchase of the mini-bus, in one of our 'operation discovery' we transported street-gangs and boys and girls each week to Holmesburg Prison, to see the prison wards, interview the inmates, and to get a realistic look at prison life. They were also taken to Philadelphia General Hospital to the paraplegic ward to interview and see some of the paralyzed gang members and to get another look at the other sides of gang warfare. Hundreds of gang members were benefited by the grant.

"... Also as a result of the grant and the purchase of the mini-bus, Neighborhood Crusades held many gospel crusades around the city. In addition, through our Night-Van Ministry we showed movies in the streets of different neighborhoods around the city. Hundreds of young people received the gospel and many of them individually expressed their appreciation for our involvement with them in taking the time to expose them to God and Jesus Christ, affording them the opportunity to receive salvation."

THE REV. MELVIN FLOYD
Neighborhood Crusades

"... We would never have been able to purchase the station wagon—so important to our work... a large blackboard was purchased... canned food was purchased... crayon and other supplies for our pre-school age children's center were purchased. Rent and utilities were caught up. Shoes were brought for children who had no shoes. We paid bus fare for a student to get to a college where she had won a scholarship, but had no fare to get to the college (we called the college first)... we bought a pair of shoes for a man with an artificial leg who had lost his check and the hospital could not replace the shoes... there are numerous human services rendered by the Rafters, because we are close to the people and from the various agencies, they come and pour their hearts out... one man came to the Rafters on crutches having suffered terrible burns on his hands, face and body; worked at night, came home just in time to see his house on fire, and his wife and children inside. He saved the entire family. Every worker and volunteer in our thrift shop gave this man and his wife funds from twenty-five cents to ten dollars. Because of your grant Rafters gave food and clothing for the entire family and twenty-five dollars to hold them until they could get a check from the compensations."

MRS. J. FLOSSIE REDDICK
The Rafters Charity

"(You gave us)... the ability to achieve our match for federal dollars and therefore, our ability to carry out our total program. A staff person from the inner city could not have been hired because we could not have paid the total salary... total program furnished counseling, location of housing, transfer of some women from jail to mental health facilities, release from jail on non-money bail, contact with judges and probation officers to obtain speedy trials, better defense, more experimental group sessions with women to find which techniques or materials were most meaningful to incarcerated women."

"... A woman was in jail for four months. During that time we contacted her family, checked on her children, found an apartment for her, bought clothes for her to wear at her trial, contacted judge and probation officer to suggest a plan for probation instead of incarceration. She was released on probation. We arranged an entry into a day drug probation, helped her move into apartment, gave her money until welfare check arrived. Counseled with her, helped her to understand that for the next three to four months (until she could get herself together) she should leave her children with her mother rather than attempting to care for them herself."

MRS. MARGERY L. VELIMESIS
Pennsylvania Program for Women and Girl Offenders

"The completion of the building for camping and conferences has been made possible... the use of the building by many of our churches and also churches and groups from other denominations... the buildings and grounds have been used by white groups and churches and the use of the camp and its facilities has effectively become an interracial and interdenominational operation."

W. HOWARD JONES
Pennsylvania Eastern District Camping Foundation, Inc.

"One hundred fifteen boys and young men engaged in Basketball, table tennis, social activities, checkers and competitive games with other youth groups. . . because of the grant we were able to purchase a van for transportation throughout greater Philadelphia. Athletic uniforms for those unable to purchase them and equipment were purchased through funds received.

Accredited teachers supervised classes in general education on a personal basis and adapted to individual needs. Several outstanding young men assumed positions of leadership and gained training and expertise by working with others under their guidance."

CHESTER MONTAGUE, DIRECTOR
Youth Recreation Project, St. Andrews and St. Monica

"The grants from the Restitution Fund Commission enabled us to obtain funds from another religious oriented funding source. Although the fire destroyed our communications, it prepared ten young people in different phases of communications. Three of these young people were participants in training at one of the major television stations. One is still with another station while a twelfth grade student. Another student, now graduated from our non-graded alternative educational program, is now developing production skills in the Philadelphia School System's alternative school in our area once a week. This student is now also studying at a community college and will become a student at Widner College in Chester, Pennsylvania with a four year scholarship in their "Project Prepare Special Students Program."

ALICE WALKER, DIRECTOR
ARD-Self Help Educational Center

(Through the funds from the Commission). . . Sibling "Family strengthening" services reversed institutional genocide of black families by—

A. Reuniting siblings with each other—
Children's Service, Inc. accepted five family groups with a total of twenty-two siblings (including adolescent males) who had been separately placed until coming into our care and being served as families.

B. Reuniting siblings with natural families—
Within the year, nearly half the newly placed siblings were returned to their natural parents. Children's Service, Inc. providing needed ongoing services. The two reunited family groups had five children each.

Largely because your contribution enabled us to continue

demonstrating that large family groups need not be separated, the Philadelphia Department of Public Welfare continues to refer large family groups, and Children's Service, Inc., continues to qualify for a high priority from United Fund."

MRS. WETONAH B. JONES
Children's Services, Inc.

"The grant has helped the morale. Children attending various classes realized that someone cared for their safety to and from the Guild. It has also encouraged parents of other children to permit them to participate because of the transportation that is given to the children.

At the time of the funding the Guild was without funds to secure a maxi-bus. This was made possible through the grant. Transportation of the elderly, sick and the handicapped, taking the children on programs and field trips that are beneficial to them. Due to the funds, persons have been helped by taking them to hospitals, Clinics, Churches and taking the handicapped for shopping."

STEPHEN W. SIMONS, SR.
Junior Electricians

Thus far we have dealt with responses found in the returned questionnaires related to the first four items therein, including:

1. The general values that came to the agencies' work or programs because of the grants received.
2. The failures that occurred because of (or despite) the grants, and what the commission could have done about them,
3. the specific benefits made possible through grants which would not have been possible without these grants and
4. any individual cases in which persons were helped directly in their lives because of grants from the commission.

The treatment thus far has included responses from only one group; the institutions or agencies which received grants. Of course, these are the persons who would be in the best position to evaluate and respond to the four questions put forward. Every other person who received a questionnaire was invited in the covering letter to respond to the first four items if he had knowledge or information which would permit him to do so. However, there was a paucity of response from any of the respondents other than those who worked with the agencies and from members of the commission. This was not entirely unexpected, and will be commented on later.

Responses to Item Number Five in the Questionnaire

Item number five inquires "what overall evaluation (praise and/or criticisms) based upon the activities of the Diocese of Pennsylvania or the Restitution Fund Commission do you have?" Whereas it was to be expected that the institutions' and agencies' responses would be more relevant to the first four questions, it would be logical to expect, and it is revealed as a fact, that responses to question number five have come not only from agencies and institutions, but also from priests and lay persons in the Diocese, as well as from members of the commission. These will be treated according to responses from these three categories.

Responses From Selected Participants in The Work of The Diocese of Pennsylvania

Two hundred seventy-eight clergy and lay persons were mailed questionnaires, having been selected from the Diocesan list of 'key persons in the Diocese'.[4] Seventy-three questionnaires were returned. Of these seventy-three, nineteen stated that they did not know enough about the work of the Restitution Fund Commission to give any evaluation. Included in this nineteen were seventeen priests, one sister and one layman. A fourth of the remaining questionnaires returned from this group contained statements such as "Although I do not know much about the work of the Restitution Fund Commission" or "I have limited knowledge about the results," this latter group was clear and generally full in its evaluations.*

The fifty-four remaining respondents (having subtracted the nineteen who "did not know enough about it") divide themselves into two categories. Fifty of them were positive and laudatory in their responses to the work of the Restitution Fund Commission. Four were negative in their responses.

Among the fifty who were positive in their responses to the

---

*The records show that the commission distributed five pieces of literature including three booklets and two mimeographed statements at Diocesan conventions between 1971 and 1974. During one convention a 4×8 foot display was exhibited. Other materials have been prepared and distributed to council meetings and at a number of Episcopal Churches in which members of the commission were invited to speak (interpreting the program). Of course, such a problem of lack of communication is not restricted to Episcopalians in the Diocese of Pennsylvania. This seems to be a problem with most agencies and institutions.

work of the Restitution Fund Commission another division should be made. Twenty-nine were all positive; i.e., they agreed with, praised, and in some instances, lauded the work of the RFC and had no negative amendments included in their statements. Twenty-one were positive and in many instances laudatory of the Restitution Fund Commission. However, they included an amendment which criticized something about the total process, for example the sale of church house, the use of the word 'restitution,' the response to militant groups, the division in the personnel of the Commission or some item of that kind.

Those who were all positive in their evaluations of the Restitution Fund Commission recorded the quality of work which was done by the commission, the diligence of its members, the possible effects of the work of the commission on the community, and 'the Commission as an example of a church agency exemplary in Christian Stewardship.' Samples from the twenty-nine responses in this class follow:

> 1. "...My general impression is that the Commission has been thoughtful and thorough in all its work. I know that in the eyes of some, the Commission did not go far enough while in the eyes of others, it went too far which can only mean that in actual fact it did a great deal."
>
> 2. "About all I can say is thank you for a job well done."
>
> "Finally, and most importantly, I must say that the work of the Commission was and is praiseworthy as a significant example of good Christian Stewardship. Almost all of the money coming into the program did in fact find its way into people—helping Black self-determination programs and grants. My admiration for the dedication and perseverance of the Commission members is without qualification. And this you did under very trying circumstances—schism within, criticism or "benign neglect" without." (From a member who departed the Commission.)
>
> 3. "...I also have respect for the people who have accepted responsibility of being on the Commission, especially Harold Pilgrim. I am certain that they have a much greater awareness of the needs of the Black Community than I have and it is my hope that they have expended the money in ways that will bear the fruits of dignity, self-respect and self-confidence in the lives of the people and the communities who have been the recipients...I would hope, in this time when many social programs are suffering, both from the benign-neglect of people in high places and from the effects of the financial depression, which I am sure have hit the Black community with greater force than other parts of our society, that some ways might be found to continue the fund."

4. "I am in favor of continuing the Restitution Fund Commission because as far as I know the record is beyond reproach. If the Diocese needs to cut down on the bureaucracy in the Diocese could it not be done in some way which does not remove from existence the Restitution Fund and the Commission that has served so well the intent and purposes of the fund?"

5. "The idea was great, but the funds to implement were not enough. What you did with what you had was superb."

6. "I believe that the overall idea of the Restitution Fund was one of merit. The principle of self-determination, while opposed by some, reinforced the ideal of the democratic process. It is important that our trust in our fellow men be such that we believe that they act upon their priorities as they see them. I am sure that those who administered this fund gained new insights as to the strength as well as the weakness in the many varied programs which were granted assistance."

7. "I would commend the Restitution Fund Commission for the way they have allocated the funds. I am particularly pleased that so many black students were able to receive help. I believe the committee has been beneficial to the Diocese helping us to do something positive where only negative approaches had been made in the past."

8. "Overall—great! It was, and is, right things to do! The self-determination, with funds handled as they were, is right.!"

9. ". . . I believe it brought some real help to those who shared in it. . . . I wish the Diocese would adopt and press for a real missionary program. It is needed."

10. ". . . I would conclude that there have been three benefits from the effort made by the Diocese in this direction:

A. Even though the total amounts made available to the Restitution Fund Commission were less than hoped, I would think there must be many members of the Black Community who feel as do two or three who talk to me, that this effort showed that there are members of the Episcopal Church who really care.

B. The Black Episcopalians in this Diocese who were involved with the Restitution Fund Commission learned a lot about themselves and their different points of view which were in often violent disagreement.

C. As far as I can tell, the efforts to further educate the white members of the Diocese to understand the problems of the Blacks of this area is largely a failure."

Samples below are taken from the twenty-one responses which were positive with regard to the work of the Restitution Fund Commission but critical of some other element:

1. "We opposed the concept of spending capital funds of the church as tending to weaken the whole Diocese financially. We believe the Restitution Fund Commission has made excellent use of the funds."

2. "While I was glad the fund received over five hundred thousand I regretted it was raised mostly from sales of Diocesan property. The knowledge, in advance, that such an amount would be there, took away from our ability to raise substantial funds on the local parish level. It was impossible to motivate people to the individual and organizational needs of the Restitution Fund Commission work. The name 'Restitution' instead of 'Reconciliation' turned most people off.... The parish was particularly glad to know that over thirty per cent of the funds were used to further educate black students. I heard no objections to the commissions dispersement of funds, and they are to be congratulated for their work."

3. "I always admired the coolness and the Christian behavior of the chairman of the Restitution Fund Commission, Mr. Harold L. Pilgrim, when he was under severe criticism and protest action. I feel the Diocesan Convention should have given him more protection and support in holding the line against what to me seemed radical and impossible demands upon church gifts and money.... I felt then and I still feel it was wrong to sell Church property to obtain money for the Restitution Fund. The money in my opinion should have been raised by a special appeal... There were good aspects of the Restitution Fund and I certainly was in favor of helping the good worthwhile causes, but not from a sense of guilt or necessity."

4. "...I do know that the members of the commission spent a great deal of time setting up guidelines for distribution of the funds and investigated each request carefully. I feel certain that the grants, particularly those to students, were well spent...however, I regret that representatives of a portion of the black population felt so powerless that they resigned from the Commission. I wish that this division could have been healed so that some of their recommended projects could have been supported."

5. "I personally think that the Commission responded responsibly to the needs presented to it and the intention of the Restitution Fund program. Having been an original member of the Reconciliation Task Force, I have been very interested in the way the Restitution Fund Commission operated. In general, I am very pleased with the high principles and thoughtful procedures the Commission exhibited in its work.... The only mild criticism is that the hope that internal difficulties of the members of the Commission would be overcome, and that they would get it together at one point, was unfulfilled.... But then I cannot expect a unity in the Commission that does not exist in our society."

6. "The division in the Black Community over how the fund was to operate undercut support from blacks and whites... the value of our funds for the congregations was in highlighting elements of racial subordination in our society and church."

7. "...It seems to me that the Committee has used restraint and good judgment in making grants from these funds. I was afraid that radically militant groups would be funded, and that was against my own judgment of what was good for the church and black people too. I remember resentment also at the time of formation about the word 'Restitution'. I still resent that term....I think from my limited knowledge that the fund has been well administered and well used. I would be in favor of its continuation."

8. "...In general I am in complete accord with the intent and purpose of helping Black Self-Determination Projects; especially I am supportive of helping with the education of black students. On the negative side, I was and remain opposed to the gun-at-the-head tactics of the Black Manifesto Group—thus I opposed aiding and abetting persons of this ilk in any way. I feel that the Restitution Fund Commission deserves a vote of thanks for a difficult task well done."

9. "I was one of those who voted against the establishment of the Restitution Fund. This was and remains a matter of principle with me....I am favorably impressed with the leadership of the Commission and the stewardship of the money. The activities that were funded seemed to be of a constructive nature. The leadership did not panic when it was challenged by radical elements within or without. Neither was the Commission carried away by the extravagant promises of the Convention. I believe the Convention promised far more money than it ever delivered. The Commission was wise enough to insist that grants be kept within limits of funds actually in hand. The Diocese got carried away by the emotionalism of the times, the grand stand plays plays of the black clergy, the guilt feelings of the white clergy, the leadership of the Bishop, and a general atmosphere of handwringing, breast-beating and fear. The Restitution Fund Commission did not get carried away by any of those things but simply did its job and did it well. Then the Diocese forgot all about the Commission and in the cold light of reason began to back off its commitments.... In my judgment the Diocese is to be twice blamed: One for accepting the reparations concept and committing itself to it, and again for backing off the commitment it made without any formal reversal of policy. The Restitution Fund Commission on the other hand, is deserving a praise for its hard work, wisdom, and courage."

Among the seventy-three responses there were four which were classified as negative. The first negative respondent indicates that his responses are based on hearsay. (They are thus not printed here entirely.) Two points were made. First, that "the majority of black clergymen charged with responsibility for disposing the funds were rather conservative. Therefore, they were reluctant to appropriate any amounts for costs directly relating to social change." Second, it was stated "it occurs to me that perhaps the commission was deficient in appeal machinery: i.e., perhaps there should have been procedure outlined by which a group that was refused funds would have been able to re-document its case before a higher and hopefully objective authority." [5]

The second and third negative responses follow:

> 2. "My objection... expresses the opinion of my church people who have resented the transaction from the very beginning... the efforts of the Diocese to create a fund to assist Negroes was commendable. The method of doing it was an abomination! Under the leadership of the then Bishop, the convention reacted to sell church house and used the monies for the Restitution Fund. The ploy was to avoid reaching into our own pockets. Instead we took what our predecessors gave us, and trusted to us, for the work of the Diocese. The cost of renting office space will be ours for only a few years. Then those who succeed us will have to bear the burden. (It may be that some funds were retained to underwrite the expenses of rental) ... this whole business was unethical, unprincipled. One recalls the episode in the affairs of David (2 Samuel:24). "Neither will I offer burnt offerings unto the Lord my God of that which doth cost me nothing."
>
> 3. "The Black-Improvement Program has crippled the Diocese so that any other pious work is brought to a standstill—the expenditure of a half million is the dissipation of the patrimony of the whole church. (The body given to be burned without the requisite charity for all the members avails nothing!)... I see in my congregation not an explosion of reactionary rage (I lost these on prayer book issues) but rather a slow imperceptible attrition of lethargy and uninterest. ... I think that there is unanimity in the parish on the reconciliation issue. We never gave to the program; we always resented the proram. Now as it dies we are too tired and frustrated to mark its passing... My people will probably believe, for years, that part of the money given for the church goes for it!"

Perhaps the only comment regarding the three negative responses detailed above is that they constitute three out of seventy-

---

[5] It should be noted that projects receiving grants include a number for drug control, gang control, improved adoption and placement policy, prison reform, need to release prisoners, prisoner's rights, alternative schools, etc. It should be noted that with the second point the original constitution and by-laws provide for appeals in the establishment of a committee and a process for the same.

three responses received, thus would not be taken to represent the considered judgment of the Diocese.

The fourth negative response states,... "The Restitution Fund Commission has meant that we were ordered by the special convention of 1970 to liquidate the Church House Fund, the Episcopal Residences Fund, and Miscellaneous Building and Property Funds ...Later, after the sale of church house, the Church House Fund and Episcopal Residences Fund were re-constituted." The respondent continues and indicates that the Building and Property Funds disappeared.

Inquiries made of present and past officers of the Diocesan Council indicate that the Standing Committee, The Committee on Finance and Property of the Diocesan Council, and the Diocesan Convention; which are the legal and proper agencies for control of these funds, made the decision, upon sale of the Church House Property, to place a sum of money somewhat larger than that received from Miscellaneous Building Property Funds in the Church House Fund. This was a matter of shifting funds within the Church Foundation, which is the legal responsibility of the three agencies mentioned. No loss, in fact a small gain, was realized in funds in the Church Foundation.

Among the seventy-three selected participants in the work of the Diocese of Pennsylvania whose responses to the questionnaires are discussed above are included priests, sisters, laymen and laywomen. Eighty-five percent of the group were priests. No blacks are included in the group. (All black priests are members of the Restitution Fund Commission and thus, reported in that category.)

RESPONSES FROM MEMBERS AND FORMER MEMBERS OF THE RESTITUTION FUND COMMISSION

Included in the twenty-three responses from members of the Restitution Fund Commission are four (4) responses from members who departed from the Commission. All of the responses are positive in evaluation of the work of the Commission. There is criticism of the episodes of disturbance which the Commission suffered. There is regret expressed with regard to the departing of members of the Union of Black Clergy and Laity. Regret is expressed that criticisms were allowed to weaken rather than to strengthen the bond between the Commission and the Diocese. It is stated that the Diocese has not kept faith with the Commission in moral support or in making money available.

Some sample statements from members of the Commission include:

1. "The Restitution Fund Commission served a definite, positive function by means of funding to help alleviate needs of minority and underprivileged persons."
2. "The Commission is to be commended for its high proficiency in carrying out its responsibility. As a priest of the Diocese, I can truly say that the entire cause for which the Commission came into being was well served."
3. "The Bishop and the Diocesan Council are evidently planning to terminate the Restitution Fund Commission on their own without a hearing or in-put from members of the Commission. We have presented requests for information and support to the Bishop and the Council, and in writing to both, and they ignore us!"
4. "I feel that all things considered, the Restitution Fund Commission has done an excellent job. The administration of the fund was no easy task for the majority of the members who had little or no experience in handling affairs of this nature or magnitude. . . . Especially creditable was the work of the members who served on the committee to screen and make recommendations regarding the requests and the education committee which provided aid to hundreds of college students, many of whom were in dire need and would be unable to continue in school without grants from the Commission."
5. "Nothing but the best."
6. ". . . The Diocese is to be commended for launching out on a 'road' hitherto untraveled. It must have taken much faith. The Restitution Fund Commission, too, deserves much credit for accepting the task laid on them by the Diocese. . . . In the nature of things, even in spite of extended preparation, for which the Restitution Fund Commission was vehemently criticized, there had to be a certain amount of trial and error. What this Commission member regrets is that so-called mistakes on both sides (Diocese and Restitution Fund Commission) were allowed to weaken rather than strengthen the bond between 'parent'—the Diocese, and 'child'—the Restitution Fund Commission. Consequently much of the good accomplished has been tarnished by so many questions still unanswered."
7. "Support for the education of worthy young people who might not have enjoyed so great a benefit but which brought renewed faith in the Church to deliver and an encouragement to go on to the next challenge. . . We have had no failures. . . it is regrettable that the Commission could not keep the Union

of Black Clergy and Laity within its fold. A bit more flexibility might have made it. It is praise-worthy that the Commission became more open to the problems of the 'different', 'radical', and 'strange' sectors of the Black community...it is praiseworthy that at this writing not a whisper of scandal has crossed this writer's ears.... Well done!... Thanks, praise and gratitude." (From a member who departed the Commission)

8. "The Commission, in my opinion, has done a herculean service under the most adverse conditions, including practical desertion by the Diocese, adverse criticism and attempted sabotage by some initial members and a segment of the community; basically through lack of knowledge and selfish interests...The Diocese should make more money available."
9. "The Diocese espoused, in the Restitution Fund Commission, a program of mission at home. To help those who have suffered at our hands, and who really need help, has high priority in our teachings. The Bishop and high Church councils and officials remained 'quiet as Christians' when criticisms and trials occurred. They neither inquired how they could help nor responded to calls for help. Apparently, now they are planning liquidation of the Restitution Fund Commission without inquiry or hearings and without the knowledge of the Restitution Fund Commission.... Well, the Church did make an effort. Evidently as pressures receded there was not enough spirit in the Diocese to carry the cause forward...Maybe that strength will come next time."

RESPONSES FROM THOSE WHO RECEIVED GRANTS FROM THE COMMISSION

A review of the 39 questionnaires returned by agencies and institutions which received grants shows that their overall evaluations (including praise and/or criticism) of the Restitution Fund Commission are high and include many laudatory statements. They praise the personnel, policies and practices of the Commission. They mark it as 'an agent of the Diocese which gives the impression that the Diocese cares for the community'. They indicate that the example set by the Episcopal Diocese has stimulated other religious groups to similar activity.

Samples from these agencies and institutions are:

1. "...The Commission is to be commended for a very outstanding contribution it has made to each community and each life it has touched. Through your high standards and

your methods of interview, as well as your grant, you let us know that someone cared. It gave us new hope at a time when all had failed. . . We owe a great debt to you. . . We hope that the children and parties who leave this center will remember it always as a safe, secure, exciting and stimulating learning experience. And the foundation that was built here was in part due to the Restitution Fund Commission."

2. ". . . Would commend the Restitution Fund Commission on their efforts and their distribution of funds to worthy community organizations. . . would be critical if the Commission discontinued their efforts in this area because of lack of pressure at this time from Social Activist groups."
3. "We and our membership do praise the Commission for their efforts to make funds available to organizations that do not want to be controlled by government—state or city funding."
4. ". . . Our Council holds the Restitution Fund Commission in the highest esteem. We believe that the Restitution Fund Commission cares and does something about the needs of the less fortunate who are helped by agencies."
5. "My praises are obvious and cannot be stated too emphatically. The praises are due more to the Fund than to the Diocese, I think."
6. "RFC is to be highly commended for its overall performance. We were particularly well impressed by the steps taken with us in determining our eligibility for contribution, in view of the purposes of the fund and the soundness of our proposal, and in holding us properly accountable for use of the funds made available to us."
7. "We sincerely commend the Commission for their involvement and concern in meeting and helping resolve the many problems confronting our society and all its people."
8. "Establishing the Restitution Fund Commission by the Diocese of Pennsylvania was a noteworthy and most timely action. The purpose for the expenditure of the funds was handled by all who were concerned about the plight of Black people, in an effort for an ultimate good which was long overdue. The Restitution Fund Commission doggedly explored every avenue of assistance they could render to aid students in furthering their education."
9. ". . . The Commission also gave grants for social improvement programs throughout the Philadelphia area. It is a sad thought to realize that such a worthy function as the Restitution Fund Commission is severed from the overall programs of the Diocese of Pennsylvania. . . For once we had the unique expression of man's concern for his fellows!"

10. "We praise the Lord for you and the spirit of mission that you have unselfishly committed yourselves to here at home."
11. "The Diocese, because of the leadership it has exerted, has caused other denominations to begin to have real concern for criminal justice and other inner city problems. It has also given some persons who were disillusioned and alienated a reason to maintain their religious faith. Programs such as ours are in desperate need of increasing their independence from local government, and churches should be one of our main sources of support. Women and minority groups have an extremely difficult time of convincing male authorities that they are competent and reliable enough to receive funding. The Restitution Fund Commission has helped all of us in these respects and we need you to continue to do so."
12. "My general reaction here is that the Commission did a very tough job—divide too little money among fantastic needs. The job has been done responsibly and by the agreed on standards with the highest ideals being put forth. It was unfortunate that some pulled out, but I guess the fact that more radical folks pulled out speaks to the responsible way in which the funds were allocated."
13. "The funding was a very much needed shot in the arm in the economic squeeze of 1972. Many of the community agencies were on the brink of closing. Your grant strengthened us enough to enable us to continue service to the community, whose needs are even greater in these difficult times."

The above quotations from members, some former members who departed, the agencies which received grants, and from selected participants in the work of the diocese of Pennsylvania stand on their faces as testimony with regard to the work of the Restitution Fund Commission. It should be said that excerpts from less than 40% of the positive responses were selected for inclusion. However, all four of the negative responses were included, and fully. Also included are all of the questions raised by the 21 respondents who were positive but had questions.

The RFC grants made the difference "within people and within the city" and were another opportunity for a "great church to cast its arm around a great people" in a period of great stress in the nation's history.

Chapter XVII

An agency helped by RFC can enhance comradery.

A visit from the Human Services Cooperative Project.

. . . development and sponsorship within and for the black community. . . .

The scene was at Valley Forge in 1969. The occasion was the annual meeting of the Diocese of Pennsylvania.

Presiding Bishop Dewitt in his charge to the annual meeting recommended that a group of black priests should be responsible for distribution of the previously discussed restitution funds.

Up rose Harold Pilgrim, in unprecedented action, to declare: "Bishop Dewitt, am I to understand the brains in the Diocese are wrapped in the priests only?" The Bishop responded that lay persons would be included. From that point on it was destined that Harold Pilgrim would be a member of the commission to distribute the Restitution Funds.

A Task Force appointed by the Bishop met and recommended that a group of 21 black priests, plus an equal number of lay persons, be appointed.

Father Grannum and Mr. Harold Pilgrim were nominated to head the commission. Father Grannum withdrew. Mr. Pilgrim suggested Walter Ridley, who also withdrew. Some black priests fought to just turn over all the money to one source, preferably a militant operation, to let this source handle the matter. In the end, Mr. Pilgrim was elected chairman of the Restitution Fund Commission.

Successful operation of a commission is like the fruitful action of a business. Frequently, members of a commission or a business complement each other. When this happens, there is a wide range of outreach.

In the case of the Restitution Commission, Harold Pilgrim as chairman provided the ongoing basis for stability. It was Pilgrim who was the "target" for those who had differing views, for those who "couldn't get their hands immediately on the money," and for those who simply did not see "this help from the church" as a meaningful response or for those who sought almost any incident to slacken the entire project.

Those who would fight the Restitution Fund Commission discovered in Harold Pilgrim a formidable foe, unyielding and unmoveable. But because Pilgrim could take the brunt of the opposition, others could carry the Commission load, and carry it they did.

Surely, the continuance of the Restitution Fund Commission as well as its origin was the work of many prominent and not so prominent individuals. All of these shared in this "appointment with God."

Those who opposed and, thereby because of their opposition, gave those who had to carry on more determination or made those responsible more careful, the contribution is etched. For the "gift of making dreams a reality" is deeply imbedded in the sum total of mankind and founded upon the "rock" of involvement. So it was with the Restitution Fund Commission. It is a story of many who aided a few and gave these few the strength to carry forth.

Moreover, the few most often give "life" to organizations as "image projection." The path to assess a commission is through examination of its leaders.

We look, next, at the officers and/or leaders of the Restitution Fund.

Chapter XVIII

Help that may make a difference in the future.

Learning is a very personal thing.

. . . based on the probabilities of
the present

Harold Pilgrim was born in Barbados, West Indies. He came to America at seventeen years of age and settled finally in Philadelphia. At the end of the 1920's, Harold Pilgrim was in the Army of the United States of America. He was part of the infantry and assigned to office work in the Philadelphia area. His promotion to Sergeant put him in charge of the office and gave him the background for serving the country in France and England.

Mr. Pilgrim learned well the procedures of business operations, carefulness, tenacity, and a healthy respect for handling the funds placed in his care by other people. These virtues were to stand him in good stead during his entire lifetime as he moved from one position in Philadelphia, up to another, up to another, and still up to another.

There is another happening that steeled this young man from outside the Continental United States and gave him a lifetime thirst for improvement of human relations. In the early part of 1921, he was placed in charge of a trainload of soldiers who had been honorably discharged and were being transported to their homes in Atlanta, Georgia. Harold Pilgrim found that he could be given responsibility for a trainload of soldiers being transported from New Jersey to Georgia, but he could not ride unsegregated on the return trip to New Jersey. This realization made a difference in a lifetime.

Many factors affect careers. Harold Pilgrim dreamed of pursuing the law, but marriage intervened and he took a job with the Post Office in Philadelphia, where he remained for more than 40 years. He ended on the "top rung" of the postal ladder as superintendent of the Fairmount Station.

Another example of Pilgrim's business index was the management courses which he took at Temple University and resulted in a Certificate of Management from that institution. Action deepened, and soon after Mr. Pilgrim began work in the Postal Service, he realized that many of the men with whom he shared each day seemed constantly in need of money loans. Mr. Pilgrim organized a small loan company to serve the postal workers. He gave the name Mutual Alliance Service Corporation to the small loan company. The word "Mutual" is self-explanatory and it was designed to serve the postal workers. The word "Alliance" was taken from the National Alliance of Postal Workers. Pilgrim at that time, was assigned at the 30th Street Station of the Post Office, and he insisted that the office be located nearby. So it was that the Mutual Alliance Service Corporation occupied space at 13 North 34th Street, somewhat less than three blocks away. Mr. Pilgrim served as president, without pay, for fifteen years, until a group of Philadelphia business and professional men purchased the operation.

The Restitution Fund Commission chairman recalls that his training in the Episcopal Church came early and he has remained true to his Church teachings. He is a Senior Warden and Lay Reader and has been a delegate to the Diocesan conventions for more than twenty years. He has shared in the general Triennial national conventions of the Church since 1925. In 1974, his own Church, Calvary, gave him a Certificate of Appreciation for fifty-two years of service to the denomination. Pilgrim was the first black to be elected a delegate to the general convention of the Church in Pennsylvania.

As a measure of the man, one can look at the priority he gives to people's welfare, especially to the young. Harold Pilgrim worked with the former Bureau of Child Care which, several years ago when it was the largest agency in Philadelphia, brings back to him pleasant memories. Pilgrim talks soundly about his work in trying to create a financial phase for black postal workers. Maintaining the stability of the Episcopal denomination, and particularly his own church, ranks third in his personal thoughts.

As with many leaders, Harold Pilgrim's office walls are filled with plaques and Certificates of Appreciation for services rendered. Pilgrim counts the *Citation of Honor* presented by the Citizens Committee of Philadelphia given on November 10, 1973; the *Certificate of Recognition* of the Commonwealth of Pennsylvania given by Governor Milton J. Shapp, July, 1973; and the *Certificate of Appreciation* by the Calvary Episcopal Church, presented on September 29, 1974, as being his favorite honors, among others.

Naturally, Harold Pilgrim is proud of some of the successful positions he had held. He is a modest person, who talks about his achievements only if he is pushed. . . and pushed hard.

History is a very fickle "recorder of deeds," but it seems that in the years ahead readers of these times will be told of the achievements of Philadelphia, of the Episcopal Church, Diocese of Pennsylvania and of the Restitution Fund Commission. Harold

Pilgrim will be included and probably mentioned often for two extremely significant contributions. The first is that he and his colleagues held the Restitution Fund Commission together, pursued the tasks assigned, and made a good name for the Diocese of Pennsylvania, although "the Church left the Restitution Commission." You will recall that the Church proposed first to raise $5,000,000. It secured $500,00 from the sale of a building, but no additional monies were either raised or appropriated for the Restitution Commission purposes.

Harold Pilgrim is sure to be mentioned also for his work as chairman of the new Black Museum, erected by the city of Philadelphia at a cost of more than $3,000,000 for the building, plus additional expenditures for equipment and for displays. The Black Museum, located in downtown Philadelphia and within walking distance of America's Independence Hall, sits on Richard Allen Avenue and is destined to be one of the show places of the United States.

Pilgrim's own words are: "I am after nothing, but to live in peace with the world and in accord with my conscience."

We now turn to Walter N. Ridley, Vice Chairman, Restitution Fund Commission.

Walter N. Ridley is a native of Newport News, Virginia. He was born into a family of bankers. His father and brothers at one time headed one of the largest black-owned banks in America.

Young Ridley attended Huntington High School in the Tidewater City at a time when the school was led by an educational great—Dr. L. F. Palmer—when this secondary institution was ranked nationally as one of the thirteen best high schools in the nation. The rating was done by the National Association of Secondary School Principals.

During his high school days Ridley was a debater and a student innovator. He secured his college training at Howard University and continued for his master's degree in psychology. Walter Nathaniel Ridley made history in the 1950's when he became the first black to receive a doctorate from the formerly segregated University of Virginia, founded by Thomas Jefferson. Ridley's feat was heralded widely throughout the world.

A long-time professor of psychology and education at Virginia State College, Ridley was elected and served a number of years as president of Elizabeth City State University, a component of the North Carolina Higher Education System. Upon leaving North Carolina, Dr. Ridley was named to the position of Chairman of the Division of Secondary Education at West Chester State College, where he continues as Professor of Psychology.

Ridley's educational background also included the presidency of the former 100,000-member predominately black American Teachers Association, which in 1966 merged with the National Education Association of the United States. Dr. Ridley's service to the American Teachers Association also included Secretaryship of the joint-National Educational Association Human Relations Commission that for more than twenty years led human relations progress in the teaching field in America.

Dr. Ridley enlarges his service to education as a member of the NEA Higher Education Caucus, Chairman, Board of Trustees, Higher Education Association Coalition of Southeastern Pennsylvania, which included the membership of representatives of Temple, LaSalle, Beaver, West Chester, Widner, and a number of other institutions in the area.

This background of educational competence gave Dr. Ridley a knowledge of application forms which could provide valid information upon which the Restitution Fund grants to agencies, students and others could be made intelligently.

One of the forms made up under the direction of Dr. Ridley included a questionnaire on "Values Attributable to Grants from the Restitution Fund Commission." Applicants were asked to describe the overall value of the grant to their organization in such things as aiding an overall program, aiding in plant or equipment, aiding in overcoming financial strain, improving morale among staff or participants, or other general items. Also required was to list specific items provided (purchased, rented, etc.) through use of the funds. This may include programs or personnel, etc.

Specifically, the Restitution Fund Commission's response to applications for funds asked the following information from churches, students, and other groups:

1. Name and address.
2. How long in existence?

3. Purpose for which request is being made.
4. Amount of request.
5. Percentage for salaries from the request.
   Percentage for programs and services from the request.
6. How many people benefit?
7. Age group of those benefited?
8. Other agencies petitioned.
9. Part of fund from others?
10. Fee.
11. Others doing similar work.
12. Name, address, phone—contact person.

Applicants for funds were also urged to give full information about the goals and future projections of themselves or institutions or agencies.

With this information in hand from applicants, Walter Ridley and PPP Committee gave their detailed attention to the requests for funds and presented careful recommendations to the full Restitution Fund Committee for action. It was intelligent process followed with diligence, and its academic substance made a difference in a most vital operational phase of the Restitution Fund Commission's activities.

Walter Ridley has some guidelines around which he centers his lifetime activities. These are closely associated with the Church. Among other stances, he believes that the "Church must forever have a goal to ameliorate the dichotomous treatment of people in our society, by laws, written procedures or other action." Dr. Ridley is a firm believer that "everyone in a Democracy has the right to express himself" and a "right to self-determination." The Vice-Chairman of the Restitution Fund Commission is certain that the Episcopal Church, because its actions are based, or should be based, on the Biblical word, Ten Commandments and the Golden Rule, has even a larger obligation to promote Christian treatment everywhere.

Students Vickie Fisher, Sandra Williams, Lois Jones and Sherry Brown, with Science Teacher Sandra Henderson, at the Tioga Specialized Learning Center.

This Agency Received An RFC Grant.

A core around which the Restitution Fund Commission revolved included Paul Gibson.

Raised in Massachusetts in the Boston area, Gibson came to Philadelphia following World War II. His more than twenty-six years of residence in the Philadelphia environs has been filled with service to the black sector and to the larger community.

Gibson brought to the Restitution Fund Commission a balanced personality, honed in the bureaucracy of the Federal government; catalytic caution refined in a life-long search for ideas that make a difference; and a quietness that promotes reason in approach to problems quite often surrounded by emotion and rhetoric. In the meetings of the Commission, Paul Gibson was slow to talk. His colleagues on either side of the table waited for his opinion because they knew that it would be thoughtful. He brought to the Commission's doings a "needed configuration of the possible based on the probabilities of the present."

Since before 1965 he had been head of the Post Office in Southampton in Pennsylvania. At the present time this Post Office has seventy-two employees. Paul Gibson has, for the past twenty-five years, been a very active member of the Church of the Redemption in Southampton. He is a member of the Vestry, chairman of the Mission Committee and captain of Every Member Canvass with the Diocese. Gibson has been elected a delegate for the past four years to the annual conventions.

Gibson stayed with the Commission for many reasons. Foremost among these was the judgment that the black people of Philadelphia and the vicinity had an opportunity to benefit from the work of the Commission. Gibson feels some of this potential was lost because of the division of black clergy and black laity over the Commission's procedures and efforts. This lack of working together—church and laity—within Restitution Fund Commission, and more particularly, the factor that there was little effort made to bring the groups together after the rift, continues to disturb Gibson. He hopes that progress can be made, producing harmony and togetherness of the Commission's goals, although he sees at the moment a drive to abandon the project. Guided by the philosophy that all people in their dealings must commonly use their patience with other people, Gibson hopes that the future may bring an expansion and extension of the Episcopal Church's outreach to the black community and to all minorities wherever they may be.

"The Diocese of Pennsylvania, the Episcopal Church, has too often ignored the granting of major positions of responsibilities and of larger funds to blacks and other minorities in the Church." So spoke Mrs. Nellie A. Barnes, recording secretary of the Restitution Fund Commission.

Mrs. Barnes, a continuing member of the inner circle of the Restitution Fund Commission, has brought to the Commission the gentleness of the feminine approach, aided by the directness of her lifetime work as an Insurance Analyst within the Veterans Administration of the United States government. Mrs. Barnes' probing into insurance policies and her carefulness in protecting the rights of soldiers who served their country have stood her in good stead on the Commission. She has been a plus in the examination of applications submitted to RFC for assistance.

The lady has little patience with trivia. Frequently, in the endless meetings where the major contingent of the Restitution Fund Commission talked on and on, Mrs. Barnes' voice was raised time and time again. In articulate fashion, she would urge her male cohorts in poignant words to "Get on with the business at hand," "Let's stop fooling around."

As would be expected, this member of St. Philip's Church has all her life occupied positions of responsibility in the institution. She has been on the Auxiliary Vestry and now serves on the Rector's Vestry.

Mrs. Barnes is a graduate of the Philadelphia public schools and of Bordentown Institute. She also attended Temple University for one year.

She is firm in her beliefs. One of these is that the Diocese of Pennsylvania, the Episcopal Church, has not yet begun to share its wealth of monies, talent, and opportunity properly with all of the parishioners, and especially with those of lesser stature be they black or white. The Recording Secretary sees this obligation of the Diocese as a new task for the future.

Father Kenneth Grannum remained with the Restitution Fund Commission.

While other prominent members of the clergy left the Restitution Commission early in what must be now labeled the famous "Philadelphia black Episcopalian split," Father Grannum remained to give his presence and his guidance to the work. His efforts helped to keep the Commission on an even keel, and his, along with the action of others, counted on the affirmative side of the endeavor.

The Very Reverend Mr. Grannum holds the personal conviction based on Biblical background that "God intends us to be together." He would have much preferred that the Restitution Commission program be a Church-wide movement rather than the consideration of blackness which developed. Nonetheless, he counts the record of the Restitution Commission constructive and believes that the production under the circumstances of the division was beneficial. It was Father Kenneth Grannum and Al Dorsey who on January 25, 1970, were the co-conveners of the first meeting of the Commission and of its predecessor committee. Reverend Grannum, Dr. Ridley, and Mr. Pilgrim were the members of the original group. This opening meeting was called to select representatives.

The Dean of Southward Deanery's coming to Philadelphia was almost an accident. Father Grannum attended the public law schools of Barbados, and did his ministerial training in Oxford, England, with the Cowley fathers. He came to Philadelphia in 1956 to visit a relative and while here served as substitute preacher at St. Philip's Church. When Father James D. Harewood, then rector, retired, the church extended a call to Mr. Grannum which was accepted. He began his service in St. Philip's Church in September, 1956.

Father Grannum talks in staccato terms about his severe disappointment over the cleavage which developed in the Restitution Fund Commission. The priest believes that the other members of the Diocese, especially persons of wealth, then hesitated to support the Commission with the excuse that "they (the blacks) have divided the Commission and emasculated its hopes and effective work." Father Grannum asked plaintively, "Why do people self-destruct in the face of so enormous a challenge?" Expanding further, Father Grannum describes the "black Church" and the "white Church" as "doing their own thing" separately when togetherness enhances power.

The clergyman of the core group of the Restitution Fund Commission declares constantly "with God, everything is possible."

William A. Scott of St. Luke's Parish, Germantown, a teacher of vocational education in the Philadelphia schools, and native of Greenbay, Virginia, has been active in his community as President of his civic association and in election procedures and processes. He was the first chairman of the committee for Plans, Projects and Priorities, and led the Commission in the establishment of criteria employed for evaluating projects and the establishment of the operating philosophy and levels of priorities. He served as Parliamentarian for the Commission. He finally left the Commission because of the press of personal and professional responsibilities, especially his pursuit of studies at Temple University.

Charles W. Polk, a West Philadelphia businessman and Ms. Lillian Booker, a teacher, came to the Commission as members during the last two or three years as replacements for representatives of St. Monica and St. Andrew's and St. Simon the Cyrenian respectively. They were ardent and dedicated members of the Commission and contributed to its work during their tenure.

John H. Bamber, representing Christ and St. Michael's Parish, was an original member of the Commission. He contributed much to the work of the Commission especially to that of the Education Committee, before leaving the Commission after two years. Another supportive member who came to the Commission in its latter days was the Reverend William G. Johnson, who came from New Jersey to be Rector at St. Andrew's and St. Monica. Father Matthew W. Davis whom Father Johnson succeeded at St. Andrew's and St. Monica and Harold May of Trinity Church, Gulph Mills, gave their services to the Restitution Fund Commission with relative consistency and remained supportive of the program as carried out.

Elected in the turmoil and widely labeled as a conservative, Arthur Slater has been "good" for the Restitution Fund Commission.

Indeed, this Philadelphia native is a resident of the "City of Brotherly Love." All his life—which adds up to half a century—has been the "prod," adding the needed essential quality of carefulness to almost everything the Commission did. Slater's insistent and incessant questions of "Why?, Why?, Why?" provided the adequate measure of thinking, time, and consideration so essential to success in volunteer movements like the Restitution Fund Commission and so vital in the preparation and recording activities that make future reporting less difficult. Even on the smallest items that the Commission faced, Slater asked the questions that caused "probing into the heart of the matter," and that provided the added ingredient to perpetuate the Commission's activities. This enabled the prophetic searching for what is right, and the priestly movements guided by 'mercy, tempered with truth" that followed.

Undoubtedly, Slater's position as a Systems Analyst at the Department of Defense with the United States Government helped in the formation of evaluations. Included was "why applicants asked for assistance," and more importantly, "how the Commission determined that the applicant ought to be funded." Should the Commission place its faith in the written words of the applicants, as well as the face-to-face review when the Commission visited a project before finally submitting the application to the total Commission, were also factors.

Arthur Slater attended Temple University and his work with colleagues and younger college men in the Kappa Alpha Psi Fraternity has never let him forget the value of training, or the need for assisting those who would be trained or the absolute necessity of guidance "to make a whole people well." With this philosophy, Slater found it easy to remain on the Commission when conservative friends, particularly the priests all around him, left the Commission and the fray. The treasurer of the Educational Commission of the Restitution Fund Commission has, since early childhood, been a strong believer in the Episcopal faith. He can count more than thirty-six years of membership in and service to

St. Augustine's Church of the Convent. For the last ten years he has served also as the rector's warden of the church.

Arthur Slater is considerably upset that the clergy abandoned the Commission and thereby relinquished the opportunity to affect the future lives of a host of individuals, agencies and organizations. To Slater, this departure not only left the Commission in the "most awkward of awkward positions," but the leaving by the clergy bordered on the unchristian. Slater is not bitter; he is disappointed that so great an opportunity was not seized also by the clergy, leaving leaders in charge of a "new movement for a new response."

The words "try to take a conscionable attitude" are often on Slater's lips. The Commission, he believes, has kept the faith. The Commission, he realizes, could have perpetuated itself by investing the money and spending the interest or kept itself permanently in office through other ways. That it has not done so, Slater feels, is rightly within the long-established position of "doing the job" and getting on to other things.

Slater, a member of the Commission from the earliest days of the appointment by the Bishop setting the whole project in motion for Diocesan approval, believes strongly that the Restitution Fund Commission is one of the things that the Diocese of Pennsylvania has done in this century that is really important. Future history will record, he contends, that through this action the Episcopal Church reached the highest level of its assistance to "brothers in need," so much a part of the Christian Doctrine.

For the future, this Commission member insists that the Church should evaluate its actions based on the input of the Restitution Fund Commission and seek actively to expand human brotherhood in our times.

Included also among those who have been constantly active and supportive of the Restitution Fund Commission are two priests who are brothers.

The Very Reverend Thomas Wilson Sterling Logan, S.T.M., is a native of Philadelphia, who cares about his city.

Father Logan has brought to the Commission the single-mindedness of the determined citizen. His volitable, stubborn sense of obligation to duty has assisted the Commission to "live up" to its promise of genuine help to people.

A member of the original group of the Restitution Fund, Father Logan installed the officers of the Commission at its organizational meeting. Mr. Logan has been active in the Commission's operations during the entire period of the Restitution Fund's existence.

He was educated in the Public Schools of Philadelphia, graduating from Central High School, in 1931, Lincoln University in 1935, and the General Theological Seminary in 1938. He did graduate work at the Philadelphia Divinity School, and received his S.T.M. in 1941.

After serving as Curate of St. Phillip's Church, New York, a year and a half, Father Logan was appointed Vicar of St. Michael and All Angels Chapel, Philadelphia in 1940. After five and one half successful years there, St. Michael's was merged with Calvary Church, N.L. on September 1, 1945. He has been the Rector of Calvary since 1945.

Father Logan's ministry has included a broad spectrum of community services. He is Past Grand Master of Prince Hall Masons of Pennsylvania, and Past Grand Chaplain of the Royal Arch Masons of Pennsylvania. He is a 32nd degree Mason, a member of Alpha Phi Alpha Fraternity, Past Chaplain of National Alpha Phi Alpha Fraternity, a member of the Emblem Club of the Christian Street Y.M.C.A., and a Past President of Frontiers of America Club, Inc.

Father John R. Logan succeeded his father as the second rector of St. Simon the Cyrenian Church in 1957, thus making for 67 years of continuous priesthood at this church by the father and son. A product of Lincoln University and Philadelphia Divinity School, Father John Logan has served on the standing committee and the Executive Council of the Diocese and served many functions on the Board of the St. John's Settlement House, the Y.M.C.A.

and the N.A.A.C.P. A third priest, Father Oscar E. Holder has been constant and active in his support of the Restitution Fund Commission. A native of Philadelphia and a product of Lincoln University and Philadelphia Divinity School, Father Holder served in several charges before becoming the College Chaplain at West Virginia State College and an army chaplain. He served as priest at St. Barnabas and the Chapel of the Holy Communion in Philadelphia, and was early appointed the Commission's historian. He is a member of the Committee on historical record.

Father Charles L. Poindexter, co-rector of St. Luke's Church, Germantown has been active on the Restitution Fund Commission during its entire existence, but with a short period of interruption. A native of Richmond, Virginia, Father Poindexter attended West Virginia State University and the Philadelphia Divinity School. He served in several parishes in New York and Hartford before coming to Pennsylvania. He serves as the headmaster of St. Barnabas School and has been elected as Dean of the Germantown Convocation.

The Reverend William D. Turner, rector of St. Augustine's Church of the Covenant matches Chairman Pilgrim and Secretary Nellie Barnes in making the third person elected to an office at the first meeting of the Commission and being retained in that office during the entire period to the present. He has served as treasurer of the Restitution Fund Commission since its organization. Father Turner, son of the Reverend Richard M. Turner, was born in Charlestown, South Carolina. A product of St. Augustine's College (North Carolina), Bishop Paine Divinity School and Temple University. He came to Philadelphia in 1943.

Also consistent in their support and activities with the Restitution Fund Commission have been James Blake of St. Dunstan's Parish, and Dr. Herbert I. James of St. Paul's Parish, Levittown. Mr. Blake, a supervisor in the U.S. Postal Service, was an original member of the Committee on Constitution and By-Laws, has served on the Committee of Plans, Projects and Priorities and as acting secretary on the Commission from time to time. Dr. James, a product of Hampton Institute, earned his Ph.D. in Chemistry at Clarke University in Massachusetts and is employed as an electro-chemist at the E.S.B. Research Center. He served on the Finance and Insurance Committee, and on the Committee on Plans, Projects and Priorities. He has been the Commission's representative to the Reconciliation Task Force, and has served as its chairman.

Another constant supportive and active member of the Restitution Fund Commission is Mrs. Dolores E. Dow, a Coordinator of Community Relations for the Philadelphia School Board. The mother of six children, Mrs. Dow has been politically active in voter education and with the Black Women's Political Alliance. She has served as campaign manager for several politicians on the state and national level. She succeeded William Scott as Chairman of the Committee on Plans, Projects and Priorities and has served on the Education Committee for the Commission.

Persons are products of their environment, of their training and of their experiences. What happens to institutions is a configuration established out of the personalities of the persons involved.

The final character of this Commission was affected intensely by the personages of its member-contributors. Thus, to understand the Restitution Fund Commission, why the Commission did what it did, and importantly, why it did not do what it did not do, and when it did what it did, we have looked in depth at these personalities.

Chapter XIX

At 4:40 p.m., April 3, 1974, the most devastating tornado in the history of the nation struck a 100-year-old campus.

Learning about the history of your race begins early at the Self-Help Educational Center.

God intends us
to be together. . . .

The Restitution Fund Commission has been careful to make financial reports of its operations. This is part of the genius of its operation.

The financial statement of receipts and disbursements from September 1970 through December 1974 follows:

Receipts

From Diocese of Penna.	$505,121.10	
Contributions	3,410.00	
Interest from Savings Acct.	7,505.58	
Interest from Certificate(s)	18,597.48	
Reconciliation Program	102.30	
Miscellaneous receipts	36,199.69	
Total receipts from Sept., 1970 to December 31, 1974		$570,936.15

Disbursements

September, 1970			
Officers' expenses	$ 50.00		
Office supplies	16.95		
Subscription to Panorama Magazine	6.61	$ 73.56	
November, 1970			
Cassettes for recorder	$ 14.31		
Telegrams	24.15	$ 38.46	
December, 1970			
Office supplies		$ 45.71	
January, 1971			
Office equipment (tape recorder)	$ 109.23		
Postage	6.54		
Safe Dep. Box Rental	9.00		
Office supplies	17.25		
Clerical salaries	17.50	$ 159.52	
February, 1971			
Premium on Treas. Bond	$ 125.00		
Clerical salary	8.50		
Secretary expenses	25.85	$ 159.35	
March, 1971			
Grants		$ 2,000.00	
April, 1971			
Clerical salary		$ 15.50	
Sub-total of disbursements			$ 2,492.10

Sub-total of disbursements brought forward			$ 2,492.10
May, 1971			
Clerical salary	$ 26.22		
Postage	6.42	$ 32.64	
July, 1971			
Officer expenses	$ 28.63		
Clerical salaries	26.95	$ 55.58	
August, 1971			
Grants	$ 32,000.00		
I.Y.C. Granted $3,000. They have an unused balance left of $519.50	2,480.50	$ 34,480.50	
September, 1971			
Grants	$ 5,000.00		
Clerical salary	8.22		
Investigator	12.50		
Chairman's expenses	12.98		
Photographs	42.50	$ 5,076.20	
October, 1971			
Grants	$ 35,000.00		
Clerical salaries	24.17		
Investigator	300.00		
Scholarship to Brenda Edwards & Cheyney College	150.00	$ 35,474.17	
November, 1971			
Educational Fund	$ 10,000.00		
Clerical salaries	36.07		
Photographs	56.50		
Secretary expenses	26.62	$ 10,119.19	
December, 1971			
Grant		$ 850.00	
January, 1972			
Grants	$ 12,500.00		
Educational Fund	10,000.00		
Office supplies	33.99		
Clerical salaries	17.40		
Printing of Constitution & By-laws	816.00		
Reconciliation Sunday	520.00		
Telephone & Telegrams	9.35		
Safe Deposit box rental	9.00		
Sub-total of disbursements			$112,486.12

Sub-total of disbursements brought forward			$112,486.12
Printing	30.00		
Office expenses	91.09		
Premium on Treas. bond	125.00		
Officer expenses	3.45	$ 24,155.28	
February, 1972			
Clients	$ 10,000.00		
Clerical salaries	79.45		
Investigator	300.00	$ 10,379.45	
April, 1972			
Office supplies	$ 7.58		
Clerical salaries	6.00		
Investigator	200.00		
Postage	20.80		
Telephone	21.73	$ 256.11	
May, 1972			
Office supplies	$ 82.97		
Clerical salaries	281.15		
Grants	48,500.00		
Educational Fund	10,000.00		
Office expenses	25.00		
Postage	100.00		
Printing	30.00		
Telephone	28.00	$ 59,047.12	
June, 1972			
Educational Fund	$ 20,000.00		
Office supplies	4.22	$ 20,004.22	
July, 1972			
Grants	$ 37,124.27		
Office supplies	3.93		
Clerical Salaries	18.15		
Postage meter rental	23.85	$ 37,170.20	
September, 1972			
Grants	$ 7,000.00		
Educational Fund	10,000.00		
Clerical salaries	80.00		
Printing	190.00		
Postage meter rental	23.85		
Telephone	16.33	$ 17,310.18	
October, 1972			
Clerical salary	$ 57.37		
Printing	125.00		
Sub-total of disbursements			$257,085.31

Sub-total of disbursements brought forward			$257,085.31
Telephone	24.73		
Office expenses	25.00		
Installation of Partition & Painting	375.00		
Electrical work	80.00	$ 687.10	
November, 1972			
Clerical salaries	$ 93.37		
Postage meter rental	23.85	$ 117.22	
December, 1972			
Supplies	$ 4.60		
Clerical salaries	25.64		
Telephone	12.43		
Photocopies	.30		
Chairman's Petty Cash Fund	25.00		
Bulletin Board used at Diocesan Convention	70.85		
Installing 2 receptacles	22.89	$ 161.71	
January, 1973			
Telephone	$ 14.00		
Postage for meter	70.00		
Chairman's revolving petty cash fund	25.00		
Safe deposit box rental	9.00		
Premium on Treas. bond	125.00		
Office equipment (Wall Clock and Adding Machine)	51.95		
Secretary's expenses	25.00		
Educational Fund	60,000.00		
Clerk's salary	28.12	$ 60,348.07	
February, 1973			
Telephone	$ 9.05		
Supplies	14.23		
Clerical salaries	53.24		
Postage meter rental	23.85		
Chairman's revolving petty cash fund	25.00		
Safe deposit box rental	9.00	$ 134.37	
March, 1973			
Office supplies	$ 12.32		
Clerical salaries	137.35	$ 149.67	
Sub-total of disbursements			$318,501.08

Sub-total of disbursements brought forward		$318,501.08
April, 1973		
Office supplies	$ 2.59	
Clerical salaries	91.87	
Telephone	27.26	
Photo copies	.30	
Chairman's revolving petty cash fund	25.00	$ 147.02
May, 1973		
Investigator	$ 100.00	
Printing	39.00	
Typewriter repairs	17.22	
Rental lease on postage meter	23.85	
Postage for meter	70.00	
Duane, Morris & Heckscher (Legal services)	80.76	
Clerical salaries	118.99	
Grants	19,500.00	$ 19,949.82
June, 1973		
Office supplies	$ 14.58	
Clerical salaries	142.12	
Telephone	22.32	
Photo copies	1.10	
Grants	35,000.00	$ 35,180.12
July, 1973		
Grants	$ 20,600.00	
Office supplies	68.45	
Clerical salaries	260.75	
Printing	140.00	
Chairman's revolving petty cash fund	25.00	$ 21,094.20
August, 1973		
Grants	$ 2,250.00	
Office supplies	26.45	
Clerical salaries	171.49	
Postage for meter	70.00	
Rental lease on postage meter	−23.85	$ 2,541.79
September, 1973		
Office supplies	$ 14.75	
Clerical salaries	47.12	
Sub-total of disbursements		$397,475.90

Sub-total of disbursements brought forward			$397,475.90
Telephone	15.47		
Chairman's revolving petty cash fund	50.00		
Office equipment (Paymaster Checkwriter)	68.90		
Bank charge for checkbook	5.74	$ 201.98	
October, 1973			
Grants	$ 26,500.00		
Clerical salaries	31.00	$ 26,531.00	
November, 1973			
Grant	$ 15,000.00		
Transferred to Educational Fund	15,000.00		
Clerical salaries	138.99		
Telephone	15.91		
Supplies	.60		
Postage meter rental	23.85		
To photographer for photos taken 11/5/73	59.00	$ 30,238.35	
December, 1973			
Grants	$ 8,050.00		
Clerical salaries	55.00		
Telephone bill	5.63		
Christmas gratuities	30.00	$ 8,140.63	
January, 1974			
Grant	$ 2,860.00		
Premium on Treasurer's bond	125.00		
Dec. telephone bill	6.74		
Clerical salary	23.22	$ 3,014.96	
February, 1974			
Office supplies	$ 3.70		
Rental lease on postage meter	19.88		
Repairs to cassette recorder	19.75		
Postage	17.36		
January telephone bill	13.25		
Chairman's revolving petty cash fund	50.00		
Clerical salaries	105.62	$ 229.56	
Sub-total of disbursements			$465,770.51

Sub-total of disbursements brought forward			$465,770.51
March, 1974			
Office supplies	$ 11.03		
Stationery	18.22		
Postage for meter	70.00		
Feb. telephone bill	7.02		
Clerical salaries	96.72	$ 202.99	
April, 1974			
Grants	$ 3,900.00		
Transferred to Educational Fund	10,000.00		
Telephone bill	12.02		
Refund on Social Security & Withholding taxes to clerks	33.25		
Clerical salaries	55.19	$ 14,000.46	
May, 1974			
Office supplies	$ 7.40		
Safe deposit box rental 1/73 to 1/75	18.00		
Rental lease postage meter	23.85		
Clerical salaries	70.00	$ 119.25	
June, 1974			
Grants	$ 13,750.00		
Transferred to Educational Fund	25,000.00		
Clerical salaries	28.00		
Janitor (Cleaning floors)	5.00		
Chairman's revolving petty cash fund	50.00	$ 38,833.00	
July, 1974			
Clerical salaries		$ 42.00	
August, 1974			
Postage meter rental	$ 23.85		
Telephone bill for April, May and June	24.31		
Supplies	2.34		
Clerical salaries	43.99	$ 94.49	
September, 1974			
Clerical salaries	$ 44.99		
Sub-total of disbursements			$519,107.69

Sub-total of disbursements brought forward			$519,107.69
Telephone bill	20.71		
1/4 ream of paper	.70		
Postage for meter	50.00	$ 116.40	
October, 1974			
Clerical salaries		$ 20.65	
November, 1974			
Clerical salaries	$ 126.28		
Office supplies	11.43		
Telephone bill for Sept. & October, 1974	15.69		
Premium on Treasurer's bond	125.00		
Rental lease on postage meter	23.85		
Dr. J. Rupert Picott (Consultant on preparing publication of activities of R.F.C.)	150.00	$ 452.25	
December, 1974			
Grants	$ 16,000.00		
Clerical salaries	133.54		
Xmas Gratuitous	25.00	$ 16,158.54	
Total Disbursements			$535,810.54
Cash balance as of December 31, 1974			$ 35,125.61

RECAPITULATION

Total receipts from Sept. 1970 to Dec. 31, 1974		$570.936.15
Disbursements		
Clerical salaries	$ 2,887.90	
Grants	355,864.77	
General expenses	7,057.87	
Transferred to Educational Fund	170,000.00	
Total disbursements from Sept., 1970 to Dec. 31, 1974		$535,810.54
Cash balance as of Dec. 31, 1974		$ 35,125.61

Respectfully submitted,
/s/
HAROLD L. PILGRIM, *Chairman*

/s/
THE REV. WILLIAM TURNER, *Treasurer*

Grants Made by Restitution Fund Commission of the Episcopal Diocese of Pennsylvania

Name	*Amount*	*Date*
Committee of 1000	$ 1,000.	March, 1971
N.A.A.C.P.	1,000.	"
I.Y.C. (Granted $3,000. they have and unused balance left of $519.50)	2,480.50	August, 1971
Institute for Black Ministers	5,000.	"
Children's Services, Inc.	20,000.	"
O.I.C.	7,000.	"
Voter Education	5,000.	September, 1971
Greater Phila. Economic Development	15,000.	"
North Central Unity	5,000.	"
A.R.D. Self-Help Center	10,000.	"
Umoja, Inc.	5,000.	"
Irwin Wardlaw (For starting a vocational school in the community)	850.	December, 1971
Black Butterfly	1,500.	January, 1972
Gray's Ferry Multi-Purpose Center	6,000.	"
St. Andrews & St. Monica (For youth community activities)	5,000.	"
Afro-American Federation	10,000.	February, 1972
Women's Christian Alliance	5,000.	May, 1972
Pa. Program for Women & Girl Offenders	6,000.	"
Sickle Cell Anemia	2,500.	"
West Park Community Development	6,000.	"
St. John's Settlement House	2,500.	"
East Frankford Day Care Center	5,000.	"
Color Graphic, Inc.	7,000.	"
Marie Lea Child Care Center	10,000.	"
Kensington Self Help Center	4,500.	"
Rafter's Charities	5,000.	July, 1972
Interested Negroes	5,000.	"
The Young Great Medical Society	3,000.	"
Robert Hoard (Tractor trailer training of men in the community)	3,135.	"
Amalagamed Plumbers	4,000.	"
Fellowship House	3,000.	"
Employment Assoc. for Re-evaluation and Training	5,000.	"
Junior Electricians	3,989.27	"
Tioga Community Youth Council	5,000.	"
*Gray's Ferry Multi-Purpose Center (Previously funded January, 1972)	4,000.	September, 1972

Prisoners Rights Council	3,000.	September, 1972
Heritage House....................	4,500.	May, 1973
Black Economic Development Conference	5,000.	"
Phila. Adult Basic Education.........	5,000.	"
*A.R.D. Self Help Center (Previously funded Oct., 1971)	5,000.	"
St. Phillips Episcopal Church (For "Just Children" a pre-school program for the community)	15,000.	June, 1973
Calvary Episcopal Church (For improving area North of Church for community use)	15,000.	"
Father Bruce Williamson (For funding of students from the Bahamas for educational assistance)	5,000.	"
Empty Foxhole	3,000.	July, 1973
Soul Shack	2,000.	"
Advocate Community Development .	6,850.	"
Nu-Cur Urban Arts Group...........	5,000.	"
Temple University Communications Workshop	6,000.	"
Bunting Friendship Freedom House .	3,500.	October, 1973
The Center—A Place To Learn.......	5,000.	"
OPEN, Inc.	3,500.	"
*Tioga Community Youth Council (Previously funded July, 1972)	2,000.	"
*Rafter's Charities (Previously funded July, 1972)	2,500.	"
Neighborhood Action Bureau........	4,000.	"
Penna. Chapter Black Panther Party .	3,000.	"
Phila. Communication Center	3,000.	"
St. Augustine's Church of the Convenant (For Gang Related activities in the community)	15,000.	November, 1973
Prison Task Force..................	550.	December, 1973
Neighborhood Crusaders............	2,500.	"
Penna. Eastern District Congress Camping Foundation.............	5,000.	"
All Souls' Church for the Deaf	2,860.	January, 1974
Human Services...................	400.	April, 1974
*Black Economic Development Conf. (Previously funded May, 1973)	3,500.	"
West Chester Community Center	3,000.	June, 1974
Sygns of Tymes	2,000.	"
Church of the Holy Apostle and the Mediator	2,750.	"

United Negro College Fund (For Wilberforce University)	6,000.	June, 1974
*Bunting Friendship Freedom House (Previously funded Oct., 1973)	1,000.	December, 1974
St. Barnabas Episcopal School	6,000.	"
The Church of the Saviour (For improving area's in church)	1,000.	"
St. Simon the Cyrenian Episcopal Church (For Pre-kindergarten nursery)	8,000.	"
Total	$355,864.77	

*Note: Funded more than once

Restitution Fund Commission
Educational Fund

Financial Statement from December, 1971—December, 1974

Receipts (From Commission)			
November, 1971	$ 10,000.00		
January, 1972	10,000.00		
May, 1972	10,000.00		
June, 1972	20,000.00		
September, 1972	10,000.00		
January, 1973	60,000.00		
November, 1973	15,000.00		
April, 1974	10,000.00		
July, 1974	25,000.00		
Total receipts			$170,000.00
Disbursements			
December, 1971			
Berean Institute (Phila.)	$ 2,826.00		
Community College of Phila.	200.00		
Temple University	245.00		
Penn State (Pittsburgh, Pa.)	200.00		
Visual Arts (N.Y., N.Y.)	250.00	$ 3,721.00	
January, 1972			
Berean Institute	$ 3,887.75		
Penn State	650.00		
P.M.C. College (Chester)	900.00		
St. Augustine College (Raleigh, N.C.)	900.00		
Westtown School (Voyage House)	1,025.00		
West Chester State College	325.00	$ 7,687.75	
February, 1972			
Cheyney State College	$ 375.00		
Temple University	300.00	$ 675.00	
March, 1972			
Community College	$ 65.00		
Boston University	200.00		
Cheyney State College	1,550.00		
Lincoln University	700.00		
Delaware State (Dover, Del.)	350.00		
Parkway Program (Phila)	250.00		
Sub-total of disbursements			$ 15,198.75

Educational Fund

Disbursements brought forward . . . . $ 15,198.75

HN Educational Center (Phila.)	506.00	$ 3,621.00	
April, 1972			
NONE			
May, 1972			
Berean Institute	$ 1,424.00		
Columbia University (N.Y.)	300.00		
West Chester State College.	1,075.88		
Community College of Phila.	1,000.00		
Hampton Institute (Va.)	300.00		
P.M.C. College (Chester, Pa.)	600.00		
Howard University	300.00		
North Carolina A.&T. College (Greensboro, N.C.)	300.00		
Michigan State University	900.00		
Upsala College (E. Orange, N.J.)	200.00		
Cheyney State College	250.00		
Eastern College (St. David, Pa.)	250.00		
Syracuse University (N.Y.).	250.00		
Temple University	3,684.00		
Drexel University	50.00		
Morehouse College Atlanta, Ga.)	342.00		
Phila. College of Art	300.00	$ 11,525.88	
June, 1972			
Lincoln University	$ 300.00		
West Chester State College.	300.00		
Carnegie-Mellon University (Pittsburgh, Pa.)	200.00		
Penn State University	300.00		
East Stroudsburg College (Pa.)	300.00		
Pierce Jr. College (Phila.)	300.00		
Hampton Institute (Va.)	300.00		
Fisk University (Tenn.)	300.00		
University of Pennsylvania.	250.00		
Bronco Junction Allergy Rehabilitation Foundation (W.Va.)	300.00	$ 2,850.00	
Sub-total of disbursements			$ 30,080.63

Educational Fund

Disbursements (Sub-total) brought forward			$ 30,080.63
July, 1972			
Michigan State University	$ 300.00		
Y.W.C.A. (Langhorne, Pa.)	220.00		
Temple University	300.00		
Cheyney State College	300.00		
West Chester State College	700.00		
University of Pittsburgh	200.00	$ 2,020.00	
August, 1972			
Temple University	$ 900.00		
Cheyney State College	2,400.00		
University of Dayton	950.00		
Phila. Office Training School	274.00		
Phila. Community College	900.00		
Gettysburg College (Pa.)	300.00		
Emerson College (Boston, Mass.)	300.00		
North Carolina A.&T. College	300.00	$ 6,324.00	
September, 1972			
Hampton Institute (Va.)	$ 300.00		
Berean Institute	7,777.00		
Messiah College (Gresham, Penna.)	600.00		
Phila. College of Art	300.00		
Lincoln University	950.00		
Pa. College of Podiatric Med.	300.00		
Community College of Phila.	960.00		
Cheyney State College	900.00		
Temple University	1,450.00		
Hartford School of Accounting (Hartford, Conn.)	300.00		
The American University (Washington, D.C.)	300.00		
Langston University (Okla.)	300.00		
Rutger's University (N.J.)	300.00		
Michigan State University	300.00		
Penn State University	200.00		
West Chester State College	360.00		
St. Joseph Preparatory School (Phila.)	300.00	$ 15,897.00	
Sub-total of disbursements			$ 54,321.63

Educational Fund

Sub-total of disbursements brought forward			$ 54,321.63
October, 1972—NONE			
November, 1972—NONE			
December, 1972—NONE			
January, 1973			
Community College of Phila.	$ 500.00		
Cheyney State College	2,190.00		
Temple University	1,200.00		
St. Augustine College	157.00		
Howard University Law School	300.00		
West Nottingham Academy	300.00		
Spring Garden Institute	300.00		
University of Pittsburgh	350.00		
Skidmore College	300.00		
Pierce Jr. College	300.00		
St. Joseph's College	600.00		
West Chester State College	871.00	$ 7,368.00	
February, 1973			
Community College of Phila.	$ 1,284.00		
West Chester State College	650.00		
Cheyney State College	1,050.00		
Fisk University	300.00		
University of Akron	300.00		
Millersville State College	300.00		
Penn State College	350.00		
X-Ray Technology School of Phila. General Hospital	300.00		
Berean Institute	300.00		
Hampton Institute	300.00		
Temple University	350.00		
Clarion State College	300.00		
Pasadena City College (Calif.)	300.00		
Dillard University	1,200.00	$ 7,284.00	
March, 1973			
Cheyney State College	$ 2,900.00		
Berean Institute	425.00		
St. Augustine's College	600.00		
West Chester State College	1,328.00		
University of Pittsburgh	150.00		
Sub-total of disbursements			$ 74,376.63

Educational Fund

Sub-total of disbursements brought forward			$ 74,376.63
Penn State University	600.00		
Community College of Phila.	300.00		
Temple University	4,585.00		
Lincoln University	1,150.00		
Rochester Inst. of Technology	300.00		
Bristol Y.V.C.A.	300.00	$ 12,638.00	
April, 1973			
Phila. College of Podiatric Medicine		$ 317.00	
May, 1973			
Morgan State College	$ 300.00		
West Chester State College.	2,445.00		
Temple University	900.00		
Cheyney State College	5,000.00		
Boston College	300.00		
Community College of Phila.	900.00		
Hampton Institute	300.00		
Tuskegee Institute	350.00		
Howard University	250.00		
Benedict College	350.00		
Duquesne University	300.00		
Syracuse University	150.00		
Indiana University of Pa.	350.00		
Lincoln Prep.	380.00		
Eastern College	600.00	$ 12,875.00	
June, 1973—NONE			
July, 1973			
West Chester State	$ 1,050.00		
Community College of Phila.	2,175.00		
Phila. College of Art	300.00		
Immaculata College	400.00		
Millersville State College	150.00		
Atlantic School of Hartford.	200.00		
N.E. Business School	200.00		
Temple University	500.00		
Cheyney State College	950.00	$ 5,925.00	
August, 1973—NONE			
Sub-total of disbursements			$100,728.63

Educational Fund

Sub-total of disbursements brought forward			$100,728.63
September, 1973			
Howard University	$ 150.00		
Cabrini College	250.00		
Berean Institute	6,570.00		
Community College of Phila.	2,175.00		
University of Penna.	325.00		
N.C. Central University	200.00		
University of Maryland, Eastern Shore	200.00		
Temple University	750.00		
Delaware State College	200.00		
Antioch-Phila. University Without Walls	250.00		
Antioch-Putney Graduate School	400.00		
Drexel University	750.00		
Cornell University	150.00		
Boston Conservatory of Music	125.00		
University of South Carolina	200.00		
Albright College	200.00		
Pierce Jr. College	200.00		
Bryn Mawr College	125.00		
Cheyney State College	2,400.00		
Penn State College	500.00		
Syracuse University of Law	200.00		
Clark College	350.00		
Lincoln University	300.00		
Hahnemann Medical College	200.00	$ 17,170.00	
October, 1973—NONE			
November, 1973			
Temple University	$ 1,275.00		
University of Pittsburgh	125.00		
St. Augustine's College	200.00	$ 1,600.00	
December, 1973			
Voyage House (Reimbursement)	$ 1,000.00		
Berean Institute	675.00		
Sub-total of disbursement			$121,173.63

Educational Fund

Sub-total of disbursements brought forward			$121,173.63
Morris Brown College	200.00		
Morgan State College	200.00		
West Chester State College	1,318.00		
Community College of Phila.	300.00	$ 3,693.00	
January, 1974			
Penn State University	$ 150.00		
St. Augustine's College	300.00		
Community College of Phila.	575.00		
West Chester State College	188.00	$ 1,213.00	
February, 1974			
Combs College of Music	$ 175.00		
Temple University	150.00		
N.C. A.&T. State University	150.00		
Cheyney State College	650.00		
Phila. College of Art	200.00		
Moore College of Art	500.00		
Lincoln University	400.00	$ 2,225.00	
March, 1974			
N.C. A&T State University	$ 250.00		
Hampton Institute	300.00		
Community College of Phila.	1,950.00		
Rochester Institute of Technology	300.00		
Panhandle State College	300.00		
West Chester State College	349.00		
Temple University	2,450.00		
Lincoln University	350.00		
Gettysburg College	300.00		
Northeastern University	250.00		
Millersville State College	600.00	$ 7,399.00	
April, 1974			
Penn State University	$ 250.00		
Berean Institute	400.00		
Cheyney State College	2,600.00	$ 3,250.00	
May, 1974—NONE			
June, 1974—NONE			
Sub-total of disbursements			$137,278.63

Educational Fund

Sub-total of disbursements brought forward $137,278.63

July, 1974—NONE

August, 1974

Clarion State College ...... $	150.00	
Montgomery County Community College	150.00	
Cheyney State College	6,900.00	
St. Augustine's College	300.00	
University of Penna.	300.00	
University of Pittsburgh	450.00	
Syracuse University	300.00	
Lincoln University	200.00	
Clark College	300.00	
West Chester State	1,449.00	
Cornell University	500.00	
Phila. College of Textiles and Sciences	300.00	
Boston University	250.00	
Dowling College	300.00	$ 11,849.00

September, 1974—NONE

October, 1974

Temple University .... $	900.00	
Community College of Phila.	242.00	
Phila. College of Textiles and Sciences	300.00	
Berean Institute	7,100.00	
Lincoln University	500.00	
Boston College	300.00	$ 9,342.00

November, 1974—NONE

December, 1974—NONE

Total Disbursements to Schools from 12/71—12/74 .... $158,469.63

Cash balance as of December 31, 1974 .... $ 11,530.37

Recapitulation of Educational Fund

Total Receipts from Dec., 1971 to Dec., 1974 .... $170,000.00

Total Disbursements for same period $158,469.63

Balance as of December 31, 1974 .... $ 11,530.37

Respectfully submitted,
/s/
THE VERY REV. KENNETH O. GRANNUM
Chairman, Educational Committee

/s/
ARTHUR SLATER
Treasurer, Educational Committee

/s/
HAROLD L. PILGRIM
Chairman, Restitution Fund Commission

Recapitulation from Sept., 1970 to Dec. 31, 1974

Receipts		
From Diocese of Penna.	$505,121.10	
Contributions	3,410.00	
Interest from Savings Acc't and Certificates	26,103.06	
Reconciliation Program	102.30	
Miscellaneous receipts	36,199.69	
Total receipts		$570,936.15
Disbursements		
Grants	$355,864.77	
Grants to Schools	158,469.63	
General expenses	7,057.87	
Clerical salaries	2,887.90	
Total disbursements		$524,280.17
Cash balance as of December 31, 1974		$ 46,655.98
Note: General Fund Balance	$ 16,409,39	
Educational Fund Balance	11,530,37	
Savings Account	2,591.22	
Savings Certificate	16,125.00	
Total	$ 46,655.98	

Respectfully submitted,
/s/
HAROLD L. PILGRIM
Chairman

Epilogue:

Chapter XX

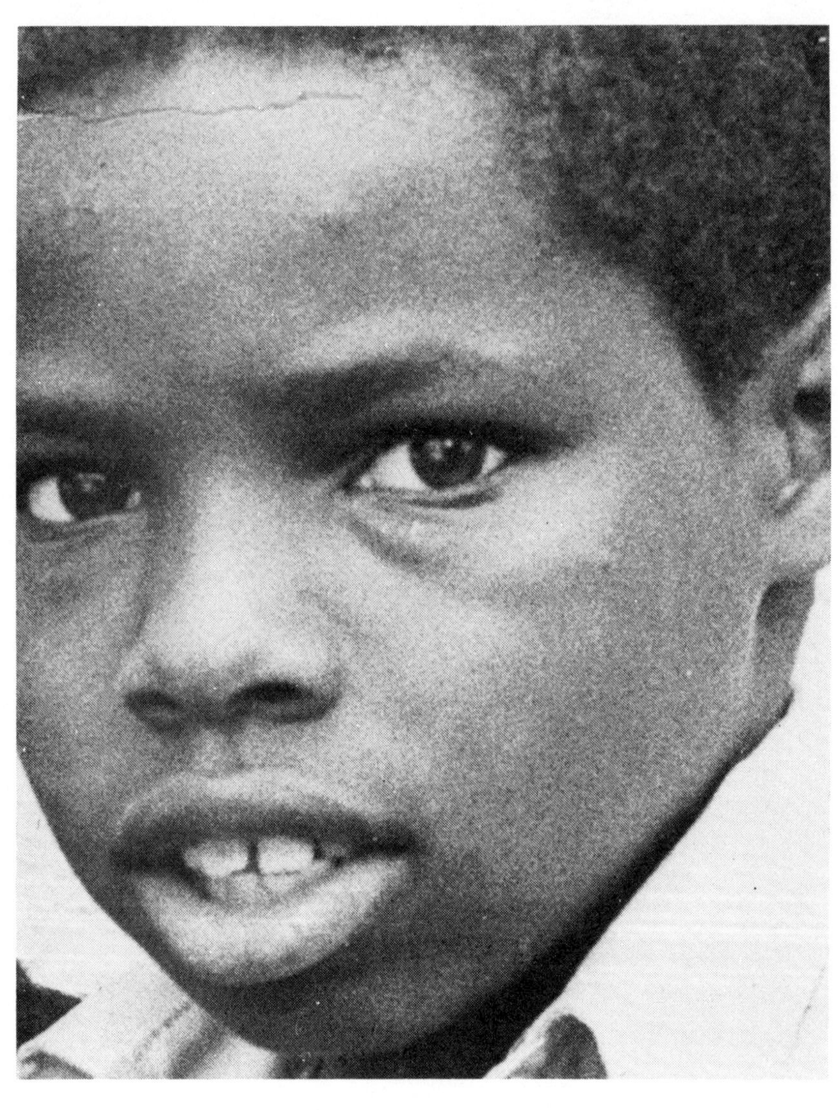

RFC worked for him and for his future.

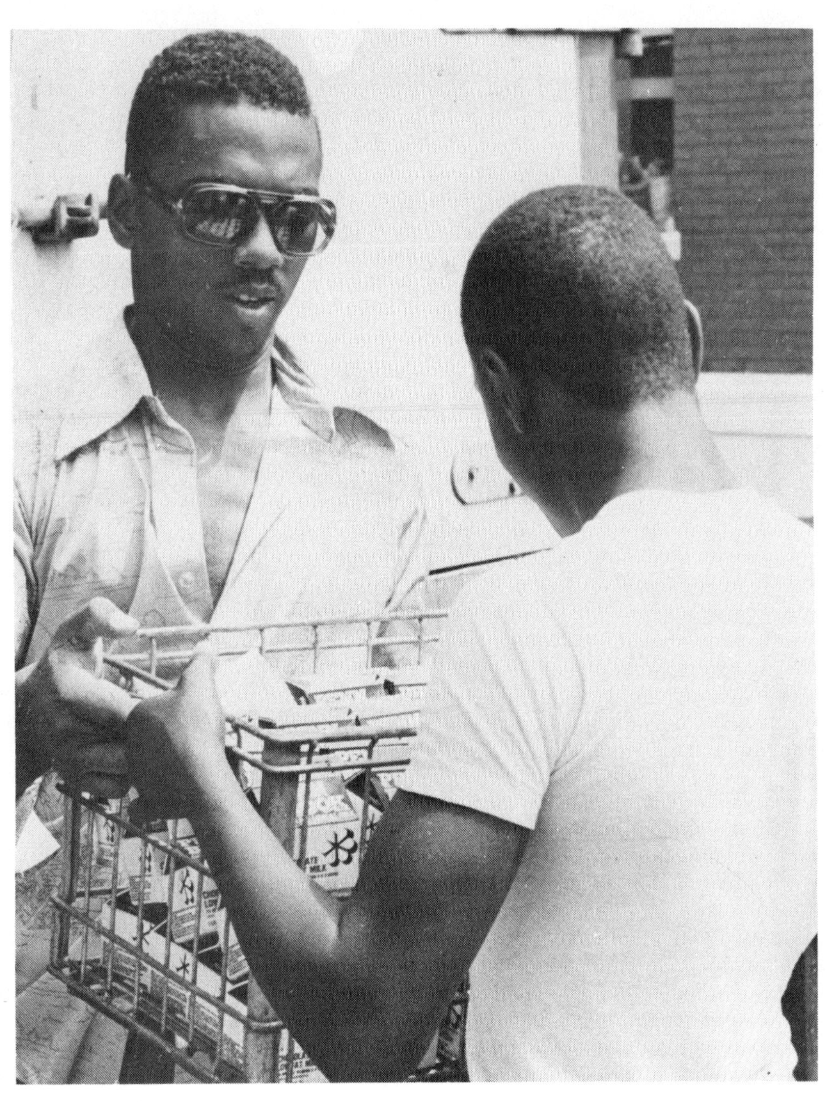

A Lunch Program pick-up.

. . . There is now a record. . .
and, from this full account,
the statement of what happened
can be made to all who may read.

The Restitution Fund Commission of the Diocese of Pennsylvania was finally a significant testament to the largess of the Episcopal Church, Diocese of Pennsylvania. That it was demanded and that it was born out of antagonism will forever be points at issue. Nonetheless, the response of the Church will for historians of the future be the determining factor. In a very real way, the Restitution Fund Commission had tremendous meaning to the Episcopalian community, and more especially, the black community of Pennsylvania.

There still are those who debate the distribution of the $500,000. Indeed, some of these individuals demanded that the money be given in one lump sum to one source by the Restitution Fund Commission. The "strings" of accounting and of ultimate reporting of how the money was to be used were not mentioned by the resisters. Suffice to say, the Restitution Fund Commission did not buy this position. It is to the everlasting credit of the Restitution Fund's business leaders' projection for the future and academic administrators' desire for tangible learning with Commission money that there is now a record, and from this full account, the statement of what happened can be made to all who may read.

Some Christians of mutuality, original members of Restitution Fund Commission, could not resolve their differences and continue to work together in God's vineyard on this project. Probably the saddest words are "that it might have been." There is no doubt that five million was envisioned for this project and only one-half million became a reality—and even that came from the sale of a building. Perhaps it was just destined to be. A case can probably be made that the Diocese never really intended to raise five million dollars for reconciliation in the black inner-city Philadelphia area. Be that as it may, the blacks who fought in the Commission and who left provided white Episcopalians with a classic built-in excuse for not raising the five million or even attempting to produce such a sum. The new words were "since the blacks can't get along," why should the whites support any side. And with this action initiated by blacks themselves, the wide potential of the Restitution Commission went down the drain... and black children and adults lost yet another opportunity to "lift their faces to the sun."

But acting within the means available, the Restitution Fund Commission did a job. This job performed is one which all can now applaud. There remains hope that someday we will learn to get along together and realize the full potential. . . if only the approach to living can be made in the spirit of the Christ, "I am my brother's keeper."

In more ways than one, the Restitution Fund Commission represented the blackness of the church. It denoted the Church's outreaching hand to some of the members who had become quite familiar with the "paucity of existence" in a large urban center filled with loneliness, despair, unemployment, and unappreciation. To these persons and to all members of the Diocese, segregation and integration, integration and segregation, are problems faced daily. The Commission became an instrument of the Church through which understanding was reached, separation of people breached, and the gap between races bridged. The Restitution Fund Commission—a new carpet—in the Episcopal Church, Diocese of Pennsylvania, deserves plaudits for this initial groundbreaking. But giant steps are needed, and the cause is imperative.

May the members of the faith in Pennsylvania and elsewhere throughout the nation and the world join anew in the solution of problems between individuals and people, so that righteousness may again prevail in our time.

Chapter XXI

RFC and the young—examples for improved human relations.

Dr. Walter N. Ridley chats with Sister Falaka Fattah and a resident at the House of Umoja.

. . . toward improved future
brotherhood for the Diocese.

The Restitution Fund Commission of the Episcopal Diocese of Pennsylvania created a Committee on Historical Record and gave it the responsibility of producing a History of The Restitution Fund Commission. It did this in recognition and full knowledge of (1) the importance of its own creation by the diocese, and of its own work to the stewardship, mission, 'do ye unto others,' and the brotherhood aspects of Christian doctrine and living, (2) the fact that the average priest or member of the Diocese of Pennsylvania knows little that is factual about the Commission and its work, (3) the fact that the Diocese, in the establishment of the Commission (and whether it succeeded or not), *may* have reached a pinnacle in its *intention* and in its *aspiration* toward its own highest ideals, and (4) the desire of the Commission that every person, and indeed every Episcopalian, in the Diocese, as well as others, review and have knowledge of its work.

The Committee has worked for eighteen months with the processes involved in this important task. It helped plan the work and has worked with the authors, reviewing and contributing as the work has progressed and developed.

This book is presented to each member of the Diocese of Pennsylvania in the hope that, as a record of past acts and functions, it will give direction toward improved future brotherhood for our diocese, Church and mankind.

THE RESTITUTION FUND COMMISSION
COMMITTEE ON HISTORICAL RECORD

MRS. NELLIE A. BARNES
PAUL D. GIBSON
THE REVEREND OSCAR E. HOLDER
ARTHUR SLATER
WALTER N. RIDLEY, CHAIRMAN

Addendum

the Center
515
A PLACE TO LEARN

An Analysis

A review reveals that the Diocese contributed $508,531.10 to the Restitution Fund Commission.

Grants made to agencies, institutions and students amount to $525,864.77. Expenses of operation of RFC and of the History have been provided by interest earned in savings accounts from funds invested while awaiting disbursement. The grants made by the Restitution Fund Commission exceed the direct contributions to the Commission by $17,333.67.

Financial Statement of Restitution Fund Commission
*January 1, 1975 through August 31, 1976**

Balance, December 31, 1974		$ 46,655.98
Receipts:		
1/75	$ 1,105.96	
1/76	1,088.58	
7/76	768.84	
		$ 2,963.38
Disbursements:		
1. Supplies and Materials	$ 121.10	
2. Clerical Services	408.91	
3. Petty Cash	50.00	
4. Treasurer's Bond	125.00	
5. Phone	169.48	
6. Postage and Meter Rental	197.88	
7. Safety Deposit Box	9.00	
8. Historical Record Committee		
a. Travel	170.68	
b. Printing (Questionnaires & envelopes)	86.06	
c. Clerical	197.50	
d. Photography	190.00	
e. Payment of two-thirds of basic contract on writing, editing and printing 5,000 copies of History	13,333,34	
		$15,058.95
9. Grants to 55 students made by Educational Committee 1/75 through 8/76	11,530.37	
		11,530.37
Balance, August 31, 1976		$23,030.04

THE REV. WILLIAM D. TURNER,
Treasurer

HAROLD L. PILGRIM,
Chairman

*This current financial statement supplements the statement appearing in Chapter XIX, which ends as of December 31, 1974.

Historical Record Committee holds one of numerous meetings with J. Rupert Picott. Left to right: Father Holder, Mr. Pilgrim, Dr. Picott, Dr. Ridley and Mr. Gibson.

Design and graphics by Lorraine Zlotnick, Incorporated

Composition by Capitol Hill Graphics, Inc., Henry Heyward, General Manager